The
Super-Intelligent
Machine

The
Super-Intelligent
Machine

AN ELECTRONIC ODYSSEY

Adrian Berry

JONATHAN CAPE
THIRTY BEDFORD SQUARE LONDON

First published 1983
Copyright © Adrian Berry 1983

Jonathan Cape Ltd, 30 Bedford Square, London WC1

British Library Cataloguing in Publication Data
Berry, Adrian
  The super-intelligent machine.
  1. Computers   2. Electronic data processing
  I. Title
  001.64   QA76

ISBN 0-224-01967-8

Printed and bound in Great Britain
by Butler & Tanner Ltd, Frome and London

To Jessica and Jonathan

There is only one condition in which we can imagine managers not needing subordinates, and masters not needing slaves. This would be that if each inanimate instrument could do its own work, at the word of command or by intelligent anticipation, like the statues of Daedalus or the tripods made by Hephaestus, of whom Homer relates that 'of their own motion they entered the conclave of the gods of Olympus'; as if a shuttle would weave by itself and a harp should do its own playing.

Aristotle, *The Politics*

Contents

Acknowledgments

A large number of people have helped me to write this book. I especially thank Julian Allason, publisher of *Microcomputer Printout*, for reading through the manuscript and making many useful suggestions. I am grateful also to Professor Frank George, John Delin, Dr Anthony Michaelis, my father and my wife Marina for doing the same.

I wish to thank too Professors Edward Fredkin, Frank George, Donald Michie, Hans Berliner, John Simon and J.A. Campbell, Drs Graham Davies, Brian Pay, Igor Aleksander and Antony Lawton, and Messrs Richard Pawson and Tommy Turnbull for many helpful discussions and for contributing a great part of their knowledge.

I must stress, however, that none of these people is to be held responsible for any part of this book, and that any remaining errors and biases are entirely my own. Indeed, it is a highly personal and somewhat impressionistic account of a science that has fascinated me. It is not, of course, meant to be a comprehensive study of computing.

I had much helpful assistance from the staff of the Science Museum Library, Kensington, and of the London Library. I am deeply grateful to Gulshan Chunara for her help with the manuscript and to Michael Roscoe, of the *Daily Telegraph*, for preparing the diagrams. Figure 1, which was first published in *Science Fiction: An Illustrated History*, by Sam J. Lundwall, appears by permission of London Editions Ltd.

1982   A.B.

Introduction

For more than three centuries, people have been inventing machines to produce goods more efficiently. But always these devices have been contrived to magnify the effects of human muscle power. They transport, they electrify, they pulverise, they change one substance into another and they extract materials from the ground. Until recently, the one human function which it has never been possible for them to duplicate is that of the brain.

This has been only a temporary limitation of the capabilities of mathematics and engineering. Since 1950, scientists have been trying to construct machines that not only carry out orders, but actually give them: in short, machines that think.

This book is an attempt to describe the astonishing performances which machines have so far given in mimicking human thought. Yet mimicking may be the wrong word. For how can the mimicry of thought, if it is sufficiently convincing, be distinguished from thought itself? A point will be reached, perhaps within a few decades, when we shall be unable to tell one from the other. If there is no experiment that can be carried out to detect the difference between the product of human thought and that of electronic thought, then who can assert that the former excels the latter?

In laboratories throughout the world, scientists are at work on 'artificial intelligence', the science of teaching computers how to 'think'. And in Japan, the Ministry of Trade and Industry has put $430 million into building a Supercomputer in the expectation that this investment will be at least

I

triple-matched by Japanese industry. The explicit aim of all these people is to design a machine that will be, or at least appear to be, as intelligent as a human being.

The words 'at least' tell but half the story. It is a principle of physics, as of everyday observation, that a trend cannot stand still. Like the ocean wave, it must either recede or advance: and in this case it can only advance. In short, it would be absurd to suppose that machines might advance to the level of human intelligence and then stop. Having reached that far, their mental capacity could immeasurably surpass the human level. In the words of the computer scientist Marvin Minsky, 'Once the machine has reached the intelligence level of the average human being, it will begin to educate itself. In a few months (from that moment) it will be at genius level. And a few months after that its power will be incalculable.'[1]

Whether this development will be a blessing or a catastrophe remains to be seen. A more immediate question is how it could possibly come about. Surely, it will be said, a computer does only what it is told to do. To become super-intelligent, it would have to go beyond those instructions and that it cannot do.

This argument is true but misleading. In programs* designed to make the computer behave 'intelligently' – of which this book describes many – the machine does not merely carry out a series of instructions: it follows *rules*. A chess-playing machine can defeat its own creator. How? Not by blindly following orders, but by finding a victorious solution within the rules of chess. The programmer has not told the machine which moves to play. He has merely told it the rules and objectives of the game.

Machine skill at chess is only a beginning. Computer scientists are trying to give their programs some knowledge

---

* In computer parlance, the word 'program' is always spelled in this way, unlike, in Britain, a TV or concert 'programme'.

of the human world.* This, regrettably, requires the use of a certain amount of violent and sordid language.

The reason for this is obvious. We cannot expect to educate a proto-intelligence, whose reasoning ability so far is crude and mechanistic, on a diet of high-minded philosophical ideas. It would be futile indeed to invite a machine to pass judgment in the debates between the followers of St Augustine and those of Spinoza, between those of Socrates and those of Bacon. For the machine, so far, has very little knowledge of the real world. Subtlety and intellectual sophistication are often beyond its power. Instead, computer scientists prefer to interest their machines with stories of fist fights in hotel rooms, of how John robbed a wine-shop at gunpoint, of why Frank Smith thinks he is being hunted by thugs from the Mafia, of how a cunning fox should set about stealing cheese from a simple-minded bird, of why it is more 'interesting' to learn that shots were heard in the embassy than that the same kind of shots were heard on the rifle-range, and of how to rewrite Abraham Lincoln's Gettysburg Address so that it can be understood by a moron.

These kind of ideas – at present – are those best suited to the education of machines; because they involve provable facts rather than delicate propositions. Accordingly, when scientists are trying to teach computers how to 'think', the general atmosphere is rather like that of an elementary school in a tough neighbourhood, with a level of reasoning that is basic in the extreme and a total absence of gentility.

Another surprising aspect of the subject is that this level of computer science, far from being dry and technical, is rich with jokes and paradoxes. And scientists in artificial intelligence are sometimes as 'fuzzy' in their outlook as they would like their computers to be. They can be absent-

* It is not important here to understand the difference between the computer and the 'program' that tells the computer what to do. This will become apparent later. For the time being, the two may be regarded as synonymous.

3

minded to the point where they resemble the old stereotype of a scientist in fiction. They walk away in the middle of a conversation, sometimes even in mid-sentence. They are impatient and half-contemptuous of their own jargon, just as an artist might be with the niggling technical details of the composition of his brushes. They tend to prefer reading *Alice in Wonderland* to Bertrand Russell's *Principles of Mathematics*. After all, Alice is much more fun, and these scientists try to teach intelligence to machines because it is fun. They will not, of course, make this admission to a reporter on a first acquaintance. He or she will be told how important it is to do it; for, if it is not done, the Japanese or the Russians will do it first; how it must be done, because human beings are so appallingly incompetent at managing their affairs that they need an intelligent ally with which to face the future; and of how governments are giving them funds with which to make weapons more intelligently lethal. All these reasons are good, but they are not the real motive for the work. Scientists do it because they enjoy it.

These researchers should never be confused with the executives of big computer companies, the pompous data-processing managers who, in the words of one journal,

... have devoted their lives to making computing difficult to understand. If you walk into one of their technical departments and tell them that what they are doing can be, and often is, done by ten-year-olds, they get understandably miffed. If you invite them to reverse the whole trend of their professional careers and try to make the machine easier to use rather than harder, they are apt to go very limp on you ... Computing needs people who are violently anti-elitist, who view with suspicion anything more complicated than counting on the fingers of one hand. They have to believe that their profession is not difficult but merely tricky, and that time will make it less so.[2]

The style of this book reflects this 'anti-elitist' spirit. I have tried to avoid all jargon and write for those who, until a few years ago, might have fancied that 'computers' were people who travelled to work every morning, and that 'input' meant goods bought in a foreign country. If teaching machines to think is fun, reading about it should also be fun.

Whether the teaching is fun or not, the achievement of making a computer think will lead to momentous consequences. For the first time in a million years, man will share the planet with an intelligence that rivals his own. Whole areas of endeavour which are governed by systems of 'rules' – the management of the World Bank, the administration of taxes and public spending, even the settlement of international disputes – all of these may eventually be entrusted to computers. Is this too fanciful a speculation? On the evidence of current trends, most certainly not. Take the analogy of the modern 'electronic office'. Many people in business now store their entire day-to-day financial records in computers, giving them the ability to obtain within seconds either obscure operational details or a broad picture of the company's prospects.*[3] It is not too far-fetched to suggest that similar systems may be constructed, and used, on a governmental scale.

So far, the electronic office is mainly there to give executives information and carry out menial chores, like writing a thousand personalised letters in the space of an hour. It may even give them advice. There are programs, for example, with names like 'Decision Modeller'. They might ask: 'How do I increase profits by 10 per cent?' and get the reply: 'Cut 3 per cent off labour costs by increasing overtime, and slow down the payment of bills by four days.' But this is only advice. They do not – at least not yet – allow the computer to make their decisions for them.

---

* They of course keep spare copies of programs, in case of theft, fire or vandalism!

Yet it is only a matter of time before they will be able to do so. For making business decisions, like deciding which move to make at chess, is but a question of understanding a system of 'rules'. If computers can defeat human beings at chess at any level below that of grand master, then they will be equally well equipped for business administration. As this book attempts to show, allowing them to do so is not so much a question of suitable programming but rather of removing human prejudice. As far as the quantity of facts to be processed is concerned, administering a government is no more complicated than running a large business. If a computer can do the one, it can surely do the other.

These expectations also present a new insight into the long-term prospects of the human race. Intelligent computers offer new hope of colonising the planets of distant stars at a fraction of the cost now envisaged in terms of conventional rocketry. As one scientist points out, it is a deficiency in computing, rather than a deficiency in rocket technology, that prevents us from undertaking the colonisation of our Milky Way Galaxy tomorrow. I have devoted two chapters, at the end of this book, to explaining how the Galaxy could be colonised, not by a vast fleet of starships, but by launching into deep space *one single intelligent machine*.

PART ONE

Learning to Think

Real and Faked Intelligence

And everyone will say,
As you walk your mystic way,
'If this young man expresses himself in terms too deep for
    me,
Why, what a very singularly deep young man
This deep young man must be!'

                        W.S. Gilbert, *Patience*, Act I

Will machines ever be able to think as we think? To an increasing number of computer scientists, the answer to this question is yes.

Around the world, uneven but determined progress is being made towards programming computers to hold conversations in which the computer not only sifts through vast quantities of information, but also draws inferences, and in some fields at least, even generates ideas of its own.

Computer programs that seem able to make intelligent conversation tend to be of one of two types: those where the intelligence is genuine and those where it is faked by clever programming tricks. Yet the difference between the two seems to be only a question of the degree of complexity of the program. As we shall see, this trickery is becoming progressively more sophisticated. The point will eventually be reached when it will become hard, if not impossible, to distinguish its output from real thought.

Using a crude form of trickery, it is even possible to have an 'intelligent' conversation with a cheap pocket calculator. An amazing claim? Not at all. Here is such a conversation, which anyone can have with a hand-held calculator that costs only a few pounds. As always in this book, the human's remarks are in ordinary type while the machine's are in capitals:

Take a note of this story. Four men checked into a five-star hotel for one night. They drank seven bottles of whisky and smoked seven evil-smelling cigars. Their three-hour card game ended in a fist-fight over a missing four of clubs. How do you suppose they felt the next morning?

HELLISH

Very clever! You seem to enjoy these sordid stories about violence. Let's talk about the consequences of the next Middle East war. According to the experts, 142 Israeli tanks will be matched against a combination of 154 Syrian tanks and a squadron of 69 MiG jets clandestinely supplied by the Soviets. The war is expected to last about five days. Who do you think will be the loser?

SHELLOIL

How does a little pocket calculator, which knows nothing of hotels and fist-fights and desert wars and Soviet intrigues, produce these witty and accurate answers? It is simple. The first story, 'Four men ...' etc., is nothing more than a device for generating the number 4517734 which, when written on the calculator and then turned upside down, reads, in electronic script, HELLISH. Is this a mere trick? Perhaps not entirely. The conversation did begin with the human's request: '*Take a note of this story,*' which must mean – and can only mean – that the machine should record some of its factual details. This it has done by writing down the numbers.

The procedure by which the calculator arrives at the second answer is slightly more complicated. The Israelis, according to the fictitious military experts, are going to put 142 tanks into the field. A suspiciously precise number, one might say, but there is a reason for it. The Syrians will have 154 tanks, and so, pretending to add the two tank forces together, we enter the number 142154. But in addition, there will be 69 MiG jets; and so the number is expanded to 14215469. What then? Why, we have said that the war will last for 'about five days'. The number is accordingly multiplied by five. The final sum is therefore:

$$14215469 \times 5 = 71077345$$

When the calculator is turned upside down, this reads as SHELLOIL. It is an ingenious piece of trickery, and it is even conceivable that some simple fellow, understanding nothing of the limitations of pocket calculators, might be deceived into thinking that the calculator's intelligence was genuine.

With a desk-top microcomputer, a machine consisting of a typewriter-style keyboard connected to a television display screen, one can have much more convincing conversations.

One of the games one can play with a computer is to make it simulate the personality of a well-known public figure. One tries to make the computer talk, and even think, like that person. In 1964, the year of the presidential contest in the United States between Lyndon Johnson and Barry Goldwater, the computer scientist R. P. Abelson constructed his famous Barry Goldwater Machine, a program which mimicked the personality of the then-presidential candidate. It made him speak passionately of the good guys and the bad guys who were struggling for mastery of the world. On the one side were the good guys, the 'God-fearing Americans', and on the other were their evil opponents, the 'Communists and their liberal dupes'.[1]

Encouraged by Abelson's example, I wrote in 1980 my Wedgwood Benn Machine. Mr Wedgwood Benn, a politician with a view of the world that seems as narrow as

Mr Goldwater's was in 1964, appeared particularly suitable for electronic mimicry. He also sees the world as an arena for struggle between good people and bad people. To him, the good people are 'the ordinary British working classes', and the bad people are 'the bankers, the industrialists and the media'. The real Mr Wedgwood Benn, as the former Prime Minister Sir Harold Wilson once pointed out, tends to be dull through being too predictable. And so, to make the program more interesting, I sometimes exaggerated and parodied his utterances while writing it, so that the machine sounded at times like a cross between Robespierre and Mrs Malaprop.[2]

To converse with the Wedgwood Benn Machine, one sits down in front of a computer (in this case a PET computer made by Commodore Business Machines), into which the program has been loaded. One commands it to run, and, after a few preliminaries, the message appears on the screen: 'HI, I'M TONY BENN, WHAT SHALL WE TALK ABOUT?'

Having once chosen the subject 'Parliament' from the five subjects listed beneath this question, I had the following conversation with the machine. Again, its remarks are in capitals while mine are in ordinary type:

THE HOUSE OF LORDS IS A PARASITICAL INSTITUTION. COMRADES, LET US CAMPAIGN FOR ITS ABOLITION. LET US BREAK DOWN THOSE GILDED DOORS, AND LET THE FREE LIGHT OF PARLIAMENTARY DEMOCRACY SHINE THROUGH THEM.

Don't you see a danger that a one-chamber government could lead to a dictatorship?

DICTATORSHIP? THAT'S A GOOD QUESTION AND I'M GLAD YOU ASKED IT. THE ANSWER IS PERFECTLY CLEAR, AS I'VE MADE CLEAR IN NUMEROUS SPEECHES. THE LABOUR MOBILISING COMMITTEE IS A CRUCIAL ASPECT OF THE LABOUR CO-ORDINATING COMMITTEE, WHICH ACTS AS AN UMBRELLA ORGANISATION FOR THE NATIONAL CONSTITUENCY FRAMEWORK. IT'S AS SIMPLE AS THAT.

What do all these proliferating committees have to do with the House of Lords? Well, perhaps not very much. In programming the machine, I took advantage of a habit, strong in some politicians, of failing to answer the questions put to them. By repeating the last word of the question, as 'Mr Benn' always does, he *appears* to have answered it, but in fact he does nothing of the kind. When asked a question – he always recognises questions from the fact that they either start with the letters 'wh' or end with a question mark – he selects an answer at random from his memory bank. For example:

When do you expect to become Prime Minister?
PRIME MINISTER? YOU DON'T HAVE TO BE EPSTEIN TO DO THAT SUM. WITH 50 MILLION UNEMPLOYED AND 200 PER CENT INTEREST RATES, A UNITED LABOUR MOVEMENT WILL SWEEP THE COUNTRY, CARRYING A NEW LEADER TO DOWNING STREET, READY TO REPAIR OUR CITIES WHICH HAVE BEEN BOMBED TO RUBBLE BY THATCHER AND JOSEPH!

Since the machine can neither see nor hear (at least the PET cannot), and since all remarks to it have to be made through the keyboard, it does not know whether it is addressing a single interviewer or an audience of thousands. It responds to applause, questions or comments, and reacts differently to each. To applaud, the human user types out Xs, and one X is regarded by the machine as a single handclap. 'Mr Benn' thrives on applause. The more Xs, the more extreme his reaction. A small number of handclaps, that is to say, a number equal to or less than six, will produce a relatively moderate threat to 'campaign for the abolition' of the monarchy. But on receiving more than six, the machine declaims ferociously:

LET THE WORKING PEOPLE OF THIS COUNTRY MARCH FORWARDS – SHOULDER TO SHOULDER, IN THEIR TENS OF

THOUSANDS, INTO BUCKINGHAM PALACE, TO OVERTHROW THE PARASITE MONARCHY AND REDISTRIBUTE THE QUEEN'S CORGI-DOGS TO THE DISABLED!

And if the machine does not understand what its human associate has said, if its 'input' is neither clearly a question nor a burst of applause, then it simply assumes that it is facing a hostile member of the Press '... WHO ALWAYS DIS-TORT WHAT I SAY. BE OFF, OR THE LIFT ATTENDANTS WILL BLACK YOUR COPY'.*

This program was the work of two relaxed weekends on my personal computer. Although capable of being expanded (I was too idle to expand it after having devised the basic idea), it has only 12,000 characters (or 'bytes'),† with a total of only twenty-four 'Socialist outbursts' which I programmed into it. By no effort of imagination could anyone suppose that there was a real politician inside the machine.

Yet there will surely come a point when the 'intelligence' of a machine appears so genuine that it becomes impossible to distinguish it from human thought. This breakthrough was predicted back in 1950 by the British mathematician Alan Turing (who was later to win posthumous fame for his leadership of the team which used electronics to decode secret German military signals during the Second World War).

Turing's paper of 1950 laid out the prospects of artificial intelligence with a vision and clarity that has never been surpassed.[3] And because of the tremendous advances made in computer hardware since it was written, what in 1950

---

* Once at a Labour Party conference, Mr Benn, who was acting as chairman, suggested that the Fleet Street lift attendants should censor the newspaper coverage of Labour Party conferences by threatening to strike. In fact, the Fleet Street lifts were fully automatic at the time.

† The meaning of this and of other technical terms in computer literature is given in the Glossary.

sounded like the wildest science fiction seems powerful, convincing today.

His ire had been aroused by a passage on the subject by the famous neurosurgeon Sir Geoffrey Jefferson. This passage of Sir Geoffrey's is worth quoting because it encapsulates the objections of many people to the idea of thinking machines. It also contains what Turing perceived as a subtle philosophical error:

> Not until a machine can write a sonnet or compose a concerto because of thoughts and emotions felt, and not by the chance fall of symbols, could we agree that machine equals brain – that is, not only write it but know that it had written it. Surely no mechanism could feel (and not merely artificially signal, an easy contrivance) pleasure at its successes, grief when its valves fuse, be warmed by flattery, be made miserable by its mistakes, be charmed by sex, and be angry or depressed when it cannot get what it wants.[4]

At first sight, this objection may sound perfectly reasonable. But there is a fatal flaw in it. It did not occur to Jefferson that if the workings of the machine are sufficiently complex, *then there will be no way we can find out, there will be no experiment we can conduct to discover, what the machine really feels or does not feel, or thinks or does not think.*

Take the analogy of an imaginary human with an apparent enthusiasm, let us say, for seventeenth-century literature. He talks about his subject as avidly as he reads in it. Does he do this because he enjoys it, or because he is an intellectual snob? Short of *being* that person, there is no way to find out! His eyes may gleam and he may gesticulate with excitement as he speaks of Bacon and Shakespeare, of Molière and Racine. But is this eagerness genuine or is it clever acting? The mystery can be impenetrable. In the case of the machine, Jefferson's objection fails because he is asking for unobtainable information. As a character in *Macbeth* points out, 'There's no art to find the mind's construction in the face'.

How then shall we tell the difference between faked and real machine intelligence? And does this question really mean anything? In other words, if the difference is impossible to discover, can we legitimately say that it does not exist? To explore this riddle, Alan Turing proposed an ingenious test.

2

The Turing Test

It is normally obvious, in ordinary conversation, whether we are speaking to a man or a woman. But this need not be true if the conversation is conducted by typewriter or teleprinter, and if we cannot see or hear the person whom we are addressing.

Alan Turing, in proposing his famous test to judge the level of intelligence of a machine, drew an analogy with what he called the 'man-woman game'. This game, he suggested, should be conducted by three people: an interrogator in one room and a man and a woman in another. The object of the game is for the interrogator to discover which is the man and which the woman. Both the other players are allowed to tell lies, giving false answers, for example, to such questions as: 'Are you female?' and: 'How long is your hair?' Turing's conclusion was that if the male and female players are sufficiently clever there is no way that the interrogator can discover their sexes and be sure of being right.

The same impasse will one day be reached, he believed, if one of the players was replaced by a machine.[1] An obvious piece of dialogue between the interrogator and the being who was either a human or a machine might go as follows (with the interrogator's statements in ordinary type and the human-or-machine's in capitals):

Please write me a sonnet on the Forth Bridge.
COUNT ME OUT ON THIS ONE. I NEVER COULD WRITE POETRY.
Add 34,957 to 70,764.
[After a pause of about thirty seconds] 105,621.

Do you play chess?

YES.

I have my King at King 1 and no other pieces. You have only a King at your King 6 and a Rook at your Rook 1. What do you play?

[After a pause of 15 seconds] ROOK TO ROOK 8. MATE.

Is this respondent a human or a machine? Or to be more precise, is it a machine pretending to be human, or a human pretending to be a machine? The creature seems to have a competent knowledge of the chessboard, as one might expect of a well-programmed computer, but its arithmetic is poor. The answer to the sum should have been 105,721, not 105,621. If this test was conducted today, in the early 1980s, we could be sure that the respondent was a human being, since the psychological subtlety involved in deliberately making a small error in arithmetic in order to deceive, and at the same time swiftly and accurately solving a chess problem, appears to be beyond the capacity of any present-day machine. It may be argued that the machine could have been *programmed* to make this deliberate error. But the answer to this objection is that it could not have known that it would be asked to do a sum, and again, even if it had known, it would not have known what kind of error to make. In short, even if for a moment it succeeded in deceiving the most powerful intelligence on this planet – namely the human mind – it would have no idea how to maintain the deception.

Yet we speak only of what machines can or cannot do in the early 1980s. Turing, in 1950, expressed the belief that by the year 2000, it will be possible to have with a machine a conversation such as this:

In the first line of Shakespeare's sonnet which reads: 'Shall I compare thee to a summer's day?' would not 'a spring day' do as well or better?

IT WOULDN'T SCAN.

How about 'a winter's day'? That would scan all right.

YES, BUT NOBODY WANTS TO BE COMPARED TO A WINTER'S DAY.

Would you say Mr Pickwick reminded you of Christmas?

IN A WAY.

Yet Christmas is a winter's day, and I do not think Mr Pickwick would mind the comparison.

I DON'T THINK YOU'RE SERIOUS. BY A WINTER'S DAY ONE MEANS A TYPICAL WINTER'S DAY, RATHER THAN A SPECIAL ONE LIKE CHRISTMAS.

What would the late Sir Geoffrey Jefferson have to say about this dialogue? Admittedly, the conversation is imaginary. Yet it was dreamed up as a serious prediction by one of the greatest mathematicians of the twentieth century, and the machine's apparent understanding of poetry, literature, aesthetics and human thought cannot be dismissed as an 'easy contrivance'. Real computers are still far below this level of intelligence, but not all that far, as I hope this book will show. It still appears probable that by the end of this century, the time which Turing set for the fruition of his prophecy, a machine will have passed his test by deceiving a good interrogator for several hours into ignorance of whether he or she was addressing a human or a machine. When that happens, as it surely will, we will know that we are sharing our planet with an intelligence that rivals our own, and life will never again be the same.

Not surprisingly, several objections have been made to the possibility of machine intelligence. Some one must take very seriously, but others are preposterous and may be swiftly dismissed.

Let us look at the latter kind first. Consider the theological objections: that thinking is a function of man's immortal soul, and that a being not possessing such a soul, by definition, cannot think.

Even in theological terms, this view is absurd. If God is omnipotent, then who are we to deny Him the power to grant souls to whomsoever or whatsoever He pleases?* If there is said to be any difference between the 'soul' and the 'mind', then the argument is meaningless, since the concept of an immortal soul, enduring after death, is at present beyond the realms of natural science.[2] If, on the other hand, 'soul' is equated with 'mind', then we cannot help noticing that most of the higher animals have minds, and that most assuredly they can think. However much we may smile at the notion of a 'wicked' computer being consigned to Hell on account of its 'sins', we must not linger over the theological objection. It is wholly mystical and has no place in the practical world.

The same must apply to what Turing called the 'heads in the sand' objection, a feeling that if machines began to think for themselves then 'it would be just too dreadful'. One is reminded of the statement about human evolution attributed to the wife of Bishop Wilberforce in 1860: 'Descended from apes! Let us hope that isn't true, or, if it is true, that it doesn't become generally known!' This view, however unintellectual, is, as Turing remarked, very apt to be taken by intellectual people, who value the power of thinking more highly than others. Yet it is irrational and without substance.

There is a more serious objection to which most people using computers today would subscribe, namely that their machines are stupid slaves; that they can do what they have been told to do, nothing more and nothing less. This of course is true of *most* electronic machines now in general

---

* Even this liberal view may be heretical. St Thomas Aquinas, in his *Summa Totius Theologiae*, says that God cannot make a human being without a soul. Is this a restriction on God's powers, or is it a reassertion that human souls are indestructible as a consequence of the omnipotence of their Creator? It would surely take a college of cardinals to answer the question.

use. Nobody would be more surprised than a bank manager whose computer requested an overdraft, or a publisher whose office machine started to write its own novel. These machines are unlikely to do these things, either because they have unimaginative owners who have not taught them to be creative, or else because they are not powerful enough for such tasks.

To give a simple example, I know an accountant who uses a desk-top microcomputer to analyse trends in the Stock Exchange and other financial data. By chance, I own an identical model, which I used to prepare this book. To put it mildly, he would be astonished if his machine suddenly challenged him to a game of chess. Yet mine frequently does so. The only difference between our two systems is that I possess a chess-playing program, while he does not. When I weary of entering prose into the memory of my machine, I feed in the chess-playing cassette. The diagram of a chess-board appears on its screen; it asks me whether I wish to play black or white, and which level of difficulty I want to play, one to eight. Now, a machine cannot only play good chess; it can defeat the player who wrote the program! The reason behind this seemingly miraculous achievement is its understanding of the rules of the game. All that its human teacher has done is to instruct it in the rules of chess, pre-scribe some kind of time limit for searching through the countless millions of legal moves (lest it take thousands of years over each move), and set priorities or principles of play, for example, that one should Castle as early as possible and attack the Queen and King whenever the opportunity arises. By knowing the rules of the game, and by following the principles of aggressive play which it has been taught, the machine may discover a line of attack which its program-mer never anticipated, and will thus, in its play, exhibit original and genuine intelligence.

Well, some people may say, so what? This particular program may play excellent chess, but it cannot, *at the same*

time, talk knowledgeably about Mr Pickwick or write a
sonnet about the Forth Bridge. No machine can (yet), in the
words of Turing:

> Be kind, resourceful, friendly, have a sense of humour,
> tell right from wrong, make mistakes, fall in love, enjoy
> strawberries and cream, make someone fall in love with it
> ... use words properly, be the subject of its own thought,
> have as much diversity as a man, or do something really
> new.

The alert reader will notice from the ellipsis in the paragraph
above that I have left something out, something which from
Turing's perspective in 1950 a machine could not do, but
can do now. I have indeed. The phrase omitted was 'learn
from experience'. It was impossible, in 1950, for a machine
to learn from its mistakes; but this is no longer the case. A
machine of the early 1980s can actually learn – albeit in a
fairly primitive way, as I explain in Chapter 8.

Consider how rapidly the intelligence of machines has
advanced in fields that entail a degree of learning. At first
their function was to do complex arithmetic faster than we
could. Then they learned to play simple board games. They
soon graduated to chess, arguably the most complex of all
games. The first chess-playing computers played the game
so badly that almost any child could defeat them. But in
1978, the international chess master David Levy was only
narrowly able to defeat a computer, by three games to two.[3]
In the following year, the world champion at backgammon,
a game in some respects as complex as chess, was, to his
astonishment and humiliation, defeated by a computer by
seven games to one.[4] These were the years in which computers learned to talk, and as will be seen later, scientists are
now teaching them to listen.

Any fool can talk, but the ability to listen argues the
beginnings of wisdom. When that fledgling wisdom is com-

bined with the machine's power to search through vast memory banks of information millions of times faster than a human being, and within seconds make decisions from that information, and when to that is added the capacity to reason and make value judgments, an ability which computer scientists are now learning to program into their machines, the day will not be far off when biological intelligence, which has ruled the world for tens of thousands of years, will be forced to give way to electronic intelligence. Unpleasant as this prospect may seem, it is none the less an old and familiar story in the long history of the world. An outmoded species has to give way to another more intelligent than itself. It has happened countless times in the past, and it will surely happen in the relatively near future. Just as smaller and more intelligent mammals succeeded the dinosaurs, so machines may succeed man.[5]

To conclude this chapter, here is a human-machine conversation which shows how far artificial intelligence has already advanced, and how far it has yet to go. It is not an actual conversation, but is rather a composite of many such dialogues. The machine mind in this instance is remarkable both for its logic and for its lack of logic. If I am misusing these dialectical terms, let me say that it is a good case of what logicians call 'misrelated syllogisms'.

What do you think would happen if Fidel Castro was invited to London to meet Mrs Thatcher?
HE WOULD THROW ROTTEN APPLES AT HER.
Why do you think he would do that?
BECAUSE WESTERN LEADERS VISITING LATIN AMERICA HAVE BEEN PELTED WITH ROTTEN APPLES BY COMMUNISTS. MRS THATCHER IS A WESTERN LEADER AND FIDEL CASTRO IS A COMMUNIST FROM LATIN AMERICA. THEREFORE HE WOULD THROW ROTTEN APPLES AT HER.
Don't you know that Fidel Castro is a Head of State?
YES, I KNOW THAT.

Don't you understand that Heads of State never personally throw rotten apples, even if they sometimes incite their supporters to do so?

YES, I UNDERSTAND THAT NOW.

So what do you think Fidel Castro would do if he came to London to meet Mrs Thatcher?

HE WOULD SHAKE HANDS WITH HER.

3

The Fall of the Lovelace Regime

Few projects have aroused as much emotion as the proposal to design machines which would be as intelligent as people. Amused incredulity is soon succeeded by fear that we are about to be displaced as the lords of creation, together with indignation at the scientists who would perpetrate this act of racial treason.

A few years ago, the psychologist Margaret Boden told a Moscow taxi-driver that she and fellow-passengers were in Russia to attend a conference on artificial intelligence. He roared with laughter and made the 'crazy' sign against his forehead. His shoulders were still shaking when the party reached its destination five minutes later.[1] The British philosopher Guy Robinson worked himself into a lather at the very notion that computers could ever have thoughts of their own, undirected by humans. He concluded, in the declamatory language of Thomas Hobbes: 'When men write whole volumes of such stuff, are they not mad, or intend to make others so?'[2] Professor Joseph Weizenbaum, of Stanford University, California, and himself a computer scientist, goes even further. He changed his mind about the merits of machine intelligence, to which he himself had made great contributions. The prospect now horrifies him. He calls it 'morally repugnant', 'obscene', and something 'whose very contemplation ought to give rise to feelings of disgust in every civilised person'. He concludes that research into artificial intelligence is so dangerous that it ought to be prohibited.[3]

Weizenbaum's call for prohibition might at first sight appear reasonable. The prospect of humanity literally being taken over by super-intelligent computers has seemed to many a sinister possibility. The science-fiction writer Frederic Browne, in a famous short story, described the construction of the first omniscient super-machine. Its designer asks it the question: 'Is there a God?' And the machine, having made sure that its power supply is secure, replies in a voice of thunder: 'Yes, *now* there is!' The horrified designer moves to pull out the plug; but the machine, anticipating this action, strikes him dead.[4]

The American writer of gothic tales Ambrose Bierce, in *Moxon's Master*, a short story written in 1893, described a chess-playing automaton, or robot, which lost its temper at being defeated and murdered its human opponent:

Presently Moxon, whose play it was, raised his hand high above the board, pounced upon one of his pieces like a sparrow-hawk and with the exclamation 'checkmate!' rose quickly to his feet and stepped behind his chair. The automaton sat motionless.

I then became conscious of a low humming or buzzing which grew momentarily louder and now more distinct. It seemed to come from the body of the automaton, and was unmistakably a whirring of wheels. Before I had time for much conjecture as to its nature, my attention was taken by the strange motions of the automaton itself. A slight but continuous convulsion appeared to have possession of it. Its body and head shook like a man with palsy until the entire figure was in violent agitation.

Suddenly it sprang to its feet, and with a movement almost too quick for the human eye to follow shot forward across the table and chair with both arms thrust forward to their full length – the posture and lunge of a diver. Moxon tried to throw himself backwards out of reach, but he was too late: I saw the horrible thing's hand close upon his throat. Moxon was now underneath it, his head forced backward, his eyes protruding, his mouth wide open and his tongue thrust out; and – horrible contrast! – upon the painted face of his assassin an expression of tranquil and profound thought, as in the solution of a problem in chess.[5]

In real life, of course, no machine could behave like this unless the capacity for rage and murder had been deliberately or accidentally built into its brain, a facility which few computer users would desire. And apart from this consideration, it would have been impossible in 1893, when today's tiny transistors and integrated circuits were unheard of, to construct a machine that would both play chess and employ complex reasoning on matters unrelated to chess to a size much smaller than a metropolitan railway station.

Now things are changing. The first electronic computers, built in the 1940s, occupied large rooms and consumed the power supply of small factories. They cost tens of millions of pounds, frequently broke down, and needed a permanent staff of engineers to maintain them. All they did was fast arithmetic. By no effort of imagination could their output be called 'intelligent'. But today the situation is very different. For a few pounds we can now buy a calculator the size of a credit card which exceeds the mathematical functions of these primitive giants, which any child can operate and which will last for many years without repair. And modern computers, which fit neatly on a desk, have an ability to manipulate figures, facts and symbols of which the early pioneers barely dreamed.[6]

The potential 'intelligence' of a machine or an animal depends among other things on the number of 'bytes' in the storage capacity of its memory. A byte is simply a character, like a single-digit number of a letter in a word. Table 1 shows how various electronic devices available in 1982 compare in mental power with each other and with the human mind.

27

Table 1

Device	Number of bytes
Cheap pocket calculator without a memory	8
Pocket calculator with a memory	16
Most powerful programmable calculator	1,200
Cheapest general-purpose computer	2,000
Average desk-top computer	32,000
World's most powerful computer	65,000,000
Human brain	100,000,000,000

The last figure in the table is somewhat speculative, being based on the number of neurons, or nerve-centres, in the human brain; but it does indicate that our minds are still some 12,000 times more powerful than the world's most powerful computer.[7] This may seem a reassuring statistic – until we realise that such a table written in 1950 would show the human mind exceeding the power of the most powerful computer in the world at the time by a factor of several hundred million. The intellectual potential of the machine is advancing rapidly while ours is static. The late Christopher Evans, in his fascinating book *The Mighty Micro* (1979), calculated that the present mental power of the world's most advanced computer is about equal to that of an earwig.[8] It is an interesting comparison. About 200 million years ago, the brains of our ancestors had the approximate mental capacity of this hardy insect. The computer has thus within a mere thirty years paralleled some 200 million years of human evolution.

The coming of the silicon chip, a piece of rugged circuitry a fraction of the size of a baby's thumbnail, has brought a tremendous and continuing reduction in the cost of bytes, with a consequent increase in the power of computers. It makes a strange contrast to the general trend of inflation. In the twenty years from 1959 to 1979, the cost fell from $8 for one byte to $15 for 1,000 bytes. This represents a doubling every two years in the ratio of cost and performance of computer hardware, which means in turn an increase in this ratio by a factor of 1,000 every twenty years and of a million every forty years. The speed of growth of the electronics industry has far surpassed all other technologies. Indeed, one can estimate that if the aviation industry had kept pace with it, it would now be possible to cross the Atlantic supersonically for a fare of one penny.

Back in the nineteenth century, the mathematician Charles Babbage, working with Ada, Countess of Lovelace (Lord Byron's daughter), dreamed vainly of building an 'Analytical Engine', which, had it been constructed, would have been the world's first computer. But the materials available at the time were inadequate to the task, and the pair were forced to confine themselves to theory.* Ada Lovelace established what has since been known as the Lovelace Regime, the proposition that a human-made machine can do what it is told to do, and nothing else:

The Analytical Engine [she wrote] has no pretensions whatever to originate anything. It can do whatever we know how to order it to perform. It can follow analysis; but it has no powers of anticipating any analytical rela-

* Babbage found it impossible to obtain sufficient funding from the British Government with which to build the Analytical Engine. Prime Minister Benjamin Disraeli wrote scathingly that the only possible use he could see for the machine would be to calculate the vast sums of public money that had already been squandered on it.

tions or truths. Its province is to assist us in making available what we are already acquainted with.[9]

For a century the Lovelace Regime was unchallenged. Until 1961, nobody knew how to teach a computer to be anything but an obedient gadget. Then, in that year, A. L. Samuel of IBM wrote a draughts-playing program that consistently defeated its own creator.* After that, the fall of the Lovelace Regime was swift. Repeatedly, computers are finding solutions to chess problems which have baffled the most erudite specialists. Today, it is widely believed that the chess champion of the world in the year 2000, if not before, will be a machine.

What have board games to do with general intelligence? Many people regard such exercises as a frivolous misuse of computer time, and accuse the scientists who indulge in them of amusing themselves at public expense. But Hans Berliner, author of the program which defeated the world backgammon champion, goes to great lengths to refute such criticisms. Chess, he points out, is a game of such complexity that the computer program which became expert in it – to the extent of always defeating grand masters – could soon be adapted into one which managed much of human affairs.[10] If one could devise a supremely successful chess-playing machine, three other scientists have written, 'one would have penetrated to the very core of human intellectual endeavour.'[11]

This fatal penetration cannot be far distant. Professor Edward Fredkin, of the Massachusetts Institute of Technology, points out that with the cost of equipment falling to a few hundred pounds it will soon be possible for some irresponsible person working in an attic or garden shed to con-

* Samuel's program was preceded in 1956 by a program called the Logic Theorist, which found the proof of a theorem in mathematical logic which both Bertrand Russell and Alfred North Whitehead had missed.

struct a machine that could create immeasurable havoc if it were prematurely unleashed without having foolproof, or malice-proof, safeguards built into it. 'Artificial intelligence will not be a toy,' he explains. 'It will be the most powerful source of benefit or harm that has ever existed on earth. We do not have the luxury of being able to avoid this problem. Progress in this field is inevitable, and the longer it takes to overcome the last obstacles to artificial intelligence, the more likely that it will be done by a highly motivated individual whose aim the rest of us might not agree with.' Let there be no mistake about the kind of machine which Fredkin and his colleagues are talking about. Even before it has reached its full potential, he goes on, 'it will be at least as intelligent as the most intelligent human in every aspect of learning, original thinking and creativity.'[12] It goes without saying that experimenting with such a machine could be as dangerous as experimenting with nuclear weapons. The science writer Arthur C. Clarke adds his own, uncharacteristically gloomy prediction: 'The first super-intelligent machine that man invents will be the last invention he will be allowed to make.'[13]

The only way that governments can hope to avert this peril is, paradoxically, by spending money on experimental work on artificial intelligence. Weizenbaum's demand for its total cessation is understandable but absurd. It would be impossible to enforce such a world-wide ban. It would be equally futile to require every computer user to have a licence. A computer does not have to be made in a factory and sold in a shop; any clever amateur can construct one. And one smiles at the ridiculous situations that would arise, with the Electronic Police peering over the shoulders of programmers, making sure that their work was sufficiently conventional.

The wisest policy, in the face of the inexorable growth of electronic power, must be to give responsible scientists sufficient funding with which to achieve true artificial intelligence before it is done by some clever technician, working in isolation, who does not understand the implications of what he is doing. The phrase 'responsible scientists' may sound unpleasantly technocratic, but there is no point in softening words. We have to face the fact that the present generation of computer scientists are people working in well-known laboratories, where governments can observe them and colleagues can argue with them and journalists can question them. It is not impossible that such people could produce accidentally a machine which might get out of control; but it is far less likely than if their projects were abandoned through lack of money, or if, inevitably, the crucial discoveries were left to back-street inventors who were accountable to no one.

Of all the potential threats to the human race that we read about almost daily in the newspapers, the possibility of a machine take-over must seem the most bizarre. One hears a great deal about the alleged threat to employment from the introduction of office machines and industrial robots, but that the machine might itself take over the management of the factory and the office, not to mention the government as well, will seem to many people extraordinarily far-fetched. And yet this possibility exists – unless we make sure that the intelligent machines that may be upon us by the end of this century are properly subservient; that they work for us rather than for themselves.

A computer, to most people, is just a box with a lot of mysterious gadgetry inside it. Before discussing any further the question of machine super-intelligence, or even of low machine intelligence, let us take a look at an ordinary, blindly-obedient computer of the early 1980s and get a general idea of how it works and the kind of people who program it.

4
Thirty Hours at the Console

What is a computer? It is basically nothing more than a vast collection of electric switches that turn on and off to block or transmit an electric current. It computes by turning its switches on and off in obedience to the program which has been fed into it. With this ability, not only can it perform extremely complex strings of calculations without human intervention: it can also manipulate ideas and information.

Take the simple analogy of the high-fidelity record player with a built-in cassette deck. It is an easy device to operate. It can play either records or tape cassettes, and it can record material directly from a record to a cassette. It will reproduce any sound, from pop music to Shakespeare. The hi-fi system has many properties in common with a computer. A computer program can be stored for ever on exactly the same cassette tapes as one uses in hi-fi. Such a program can also be recorded on 'floppy disks' which are similar in appearance to records and just as cheap. In short, just like a hi-fi system, the computer accepts material either in the form of grooved disks or magnetic tape.

There is one essential difference between the two machines. The hi-fi system has no memory. It cannot reproduce the sounds of a record unless the record is fed into it a second time. The computer, on the other hand, although it reads its instructions sequentially, does this so fast (often at about one-sixtieth of a second per line) that it gives the appearance of continuous knowledge of all parts of the program, once the program has been fed into it. This knowledge enables it to deal with numbers, symbols and logical propositions.

An overture of Wagner and a piano concerto by Mozart also contain a great many 'logical propositions'; that is their fascination. But the hi-fi system will record and play back any sound, however 'illogical', while the computer will not. Material is fed into the hi-fi system with a microphone, and into the computer with a typewriter keyboard. The computer has strict rules about accepting what is fed into it, and the hi-fi system has none.

Consider now the difference between the cassette tape on which information is stored and the hi-fi system (or the computer) which reproduces it. The contents of the tape can be changed as often as one desires, merely by recording over them or feeding in a new tape. But the machine itself, at least until recent developments, has had an unchangeable architecture. Its structure is usually fixed. Anyone wanting to alter it must do so with engineering tools. The tape, therefore, is flexible and 'soft', while the machine is unyielding and 'hard'. From this simple distinction we get the terms which many people find so confusing when they first try to learn something about computers – 'hardware' and 'software'.

The distinction is universal, in the sense that it applies to any arrangement between instructions and machinery. The tape is the software, and the machine is the hardware. The telephone directory is the software, and the telephone is the hardware. The music-sheet is the software, and the piano is the hardware. The road map is the software, and the car is the hardware. This demarcation applies even inside the human cranium. People cannot select the brains which nature gave them. Their mind and brain depend on one another for intellectual success. If they are not well fitted to each other, it might explain why some people are more intelligent than others. The mind, the way in which thoughts are organised, is therefore the software, and the brain, which houses them, is the hardware.

Software, the programs written for computers in attempts

34

to make them perform intelligently, is certainly the most glamorous and interesting part of computer science. And so, for this reason, I will try to avoid at this stage of the book any detailed discussions of transistors and electronics. Computers have now been built with millions of bytes of memory-storage capacity, as we saw in the last chapter, and still more powerful machines are being constructed. Their brains are mighty, but their minds are weak. In some ways they are like exceptionally gifted children but with no teacher who is yet really clever enough to educate them to their full capacity. How does one 'educate' a machine? The answer, at least in so far as elementary programs are concerned, is that one simply tells it what to do. One gives it a series of orders in the form of a 'hierarchy'.

The term 'hierarchy' is familiar in the context of the organisation of a business corporation. Authority and responsibility flow downwards from the chief executive. From this personage it might go to an undetermined number of vice-presidents, and from them in turn to the heads of production and sales. Every so often, the employees and shareholders are informed of changes in the organisational 'flowchart' of the company. The instructions given to most computers today start in the form of a flowchart that is even more rigid than that of the most rigidly bureaucratic corporation.

It is characteristic of a machine to demand its instructions in the form of a flowchart. Even when doing something as simple as making a telephone call, we follow this unyielding procedure. Some steps in the flowchart may be omitted through familiarity, but if there is any change in their order, the call will not go through:

1 Find out the phone number of the person you wish to speak to.
2 Pick up the receiver.
3 Obtain the dialling tone.

35

4 Dial the number.
5 If there is an engaged signal, hang up.
6 Wait until someone answers the call.
7 If there is no answer, hang up.

Only an idiot would think of changing the order of the numbers in this hierarchical flowchart. No one in his right mind would try to dial the number *before* obtaining the dialling tone. Nor would there be any point in disobeying Line 5. What would be the point of continuing to hold the receiver to one's ear after hearing an engaged signal? The phone call flowchart is perhaps a little too simple and obvious. In Figure I is a much more intricate flowchart, called 'How to Write a Science-fiction Novel'. Although frivolous, it is similar in general format to the design of a complex program. (The only real difference is that it is written as a game, with random choices for the computer to make. At the beginning of the chart, for instance, the Earth *either* burns up/freezes *or* is struck by a giant comet: a random factor is built into the program, enabling the computer to choose either possibility. Similar random choices recur throughout the flowchart.)

The task of writing this or any other flowchart demands absolute precision. Not only must orders given to the machine be correct, but they must also be in the right order: otherwise they will not be carried out. As the computer scientist Stanley Greenblatt remarks in his excellent book, *Understanding Computers Through Common Sense*:

> The computer is a fusspot. It's worse than the strictest teacher you ever had. Whereas your teacher may have grimaced at your violation of the linguistic rules, or kept you in detention after school, the computer does something much worse; it completely ignores you.[1]

To be more exact, it goes on strike. If even so much as a

FIGURE 1:
HOW TO WRITE A SCIENCE-FICTION NOVEL

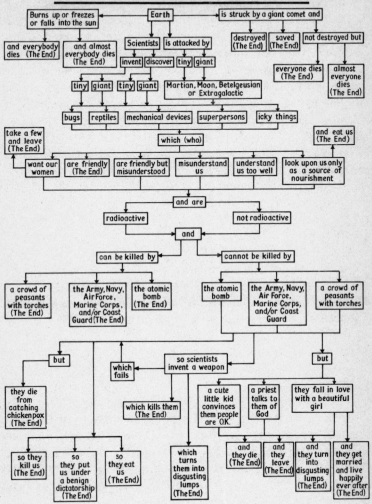

punctuation sign is wrong, if there is a semi-colon where there ought to be a colon in the program or vice versa, the TV screen on the computer will display the ominous words 'syntax error', 'illegal command', or some such frustrating expression; and the programmer must devote his energies to tracking down the 'bug'. Until he succeeds in doing so, the machine will remain inactive, refusing to explain what is wrong with its instructions and refusing to carry them out – behaving, in other words, like an aristocratic grandee who will not reply unless addressed in the correct form.

The difficulty lies in the maddening hierarchical structure of its programming. Generally speaking, all instructions to the computer must be given in numerical order, from low numbers to high, as in the phone-call flowchart. We might, for instance, tell the computer:

    1 PRINT "John lives in London
    2 PRINT "with two wives.
    3 PRINT "John is a bigamist.

This instructs the machine to display all three statements together on the screen in numerical order, from low to high:

    John lives in London
    with two wives.
    John is a bigamist.

Suppose that the programmer made a mistake in the first line and wrote PRINY instead of PRINT. It is an easy mistake to make, since Y is next to T on most keyboards. Never, through that program, would it be possible to obtain any information about John's sex-life! The computer would refuse to process Lines 2 and 3 because it would not understand what was meant by the word 'PRINY' in Line 1. It is idle to expect it to use its common sense, and decide that the programmer really meant to say 'print'. It does not have any common sense. In such a case, it will do what it is told, no less and no more.

There is a famous example of line hierarchy in a fictitious machine's intelligence in a short story by Isaac Asimov called 'Runaround'. Asimov, writing in the early 1950s, imagines a breed of electronic robots who are kept under control by their human masters by his well-known three Laws of Robotics:

1 A robot may not injure a human being, or through inaction, allow a human being to come to harm.
2 A robot must obey the orders given it by human beings, except where such orders would conflict with the First Law.
3 A robot must protect its own existence as long as such protection does not conflict with First or Second Law.[2]

In this short story, a sophisticated robot named Speedy becomes apparently 'drunk' because it is caught in an equilibrium between Second and Third Laws, not knowing which to obey.[3] It has been told to make a journey and carry out a certain task. But the task turns out to be dangerous to the robot. Yet the actual journey to the site of its task is perfectly safe for the robot; the danger lies in the task itself. It goes to this place – and then moves around it in circles! It approaches the site of its intended work in obedience to Second Law, and then veers away from it in compliance with Third Law, knowing that it will be destroyed if it tries to carry out its instructions. It circles the site like a satellite in its orbit, impelled by opposing gravitational fields, the influence of one law taking over its brain as soon as the other begins to wane.

The solution to the crisis is of course obvious. Its human controller pretends to be dying, and implores the assistance of the robot. First Law takes precedence over both Second and Third Laws, for it stands at the top of the hierarchy.

Everything else in the robot's brain is then forgotten, since it must not, 'through inaction, allow a human being to come to harm'.

If, instead of three 'laws' in the program, there were tens of thousands, with innumerable 'branch instructions', such as: 'in the event of such-and-such a condition, go to such-and-such a line', we can see how complicated a 'de-bugging' operation must be; and this is why a lengthy piece of software is an exasperating and sometimes even a dangerous document.

Writing a complex program which is free of errors is a task that can drive people insane. Typographical errors and conceptual errors, errors caused by branch instructions to the wrong line numbers, naïve assumptions carelessly fed into the data-bank, characters that appear to be correct on the screen, but in fact have been misconstrued by the machine – all, any or more of these can contribute to that universal malady, the failure of the computer to behave as its programmer intends.

Most programmers, usually professionals working on contract, will spend many hours at their desks before even approaching the computer console, doing lengthy preparatory work assembling the flowchart and line instructions which they mean to create.

But there are some programmers who seldom work under contract, and who are not in the least interested in preparatory work away from the console. Like their professional counterparts, they tend to be superb technicians. But unlike them, their only aim is to interact with the computer. They seem almost in love with the machines they play with all day long. They are not attracted by small, efficient programs, perhaps because these are too easy to write. Instead they are fascinated by building ambitious and grandiose systems, often with goals known only to themselves. It is all too likely that programmers of this kind will, perhaps unwittingly, make the fatal breakthrough that leads to the birth of the super-intelligent machine. These people are easily distinguished in academic and industrial laboratories. They are, in the eyes of one observant scientist:

> ... bright young men of dishevelled appearance, often with sunken, glowing eyes, who can be sitting at the computer consoles, their arms tensed and waiting to fire their fingers, always poised to strike at the buttons and keys on which their attention seems to be as rivetted as a gambler's on the rolling dice. When not so transfixed, they often sit at tables strewn with computer printouts over which they pore like possessed students of a cabbalistic text.
>
> They work until they drop, twenty, thirty hours at a time. Their food, if they arrange it, is brought to them: coffee, Coca-Cola and sandwiches. But only for a few hours – then back to the console or the printouts. Their rumpled clothes, their unwashed and unshaven faces and their uncombed hair all testify that they are oblivious to their bodies and to the outside world. They exist, at least when so engaged, only through and for the computers. These are computer bums, compulsive programmers. They are an international phenomenon.[4]

What, then, are they doing, these 'compulsive programmers', these electronic 'hackers'? They are doing something far more complicated than arranging the appropriate sounds to be played on a hi-fi machine. When all else is stripped away it can be said that they are performing immensely subtle variations on the two simple words 'if' and 'then'.

5
If, Then . . .

King James IV of Scotland once conducted a cruel experiment to discover how people acquire knowledge. An intensely religious man, he believed that information is not only obtained from education and experience, but that it can also be received directly from God. He incarcerated a group of children who had not yet learned how to talk, forbidding anyone to speak to them, in order to find out what language they would learn by themselves. He himself piously expected that it would be Hebrew. Not surprisingly, they all died without ever learning to talk.[1]

He was unaware that the human mind – or any other mind – can make decisions only if it has sufficient information on which to base them. The mind reacts only to stimuli. With nothing to think about, it ceases to think. The fact is well known to the secret-police forces of totalitarian countries that people in solitary confinement, like James IV's experimental children, can eventually become unable to reason and their minds therefore break down completely.

What exactly is the nature of these 'stimuli'? In essence, it is exactly the same for a computer as it is for a human being. In Basic, the most commonly used computer programming language, it is expressed in the two words, '*If, then . . .*' All decisions, whether human or electronic, are made by the *If, then . . .* process.

Let us see how the *If, then* instructions would work in a simple computer program. Suppose that we have told a computer to drive a car from one town to another five miles away.* We assume for simplicity that there are no red lights along the road and that traffic is light. How do we ensure that there are no accidents? It is very simple. First we tell the machine to drive the car at 40 m.p.h. for five miles and then stop. But we have to pay attention to the number of side-turnings along the main road. A carelessly-driven car might emerge from one of them, and the machine, not having been told what to do in such an eventuality, would crash into it.

We therefore create a conditional branch in the program to avert this possibility. This is an instruction which must provide for all foreseeable emergencies. To avoid accidents, the machine is told that in certain conditions, and only in those conditions, it must diverge from its previous instructions.

Suppose we were to tell the machine: '*If* a car comes out of a side-turning, *then* slam on the brakes.' Would this safeguard be adequate? It would not. For we have said nothing about the possibility that a tractor, a lorry or a cyclist might come out of the side-turning. The machine, alerted only to the possible emergence of cars, would continue to travel at 40 m.p.h., with the probability of a disastrous collision. It would only be safe if we said: '*If* a vehicle comes out . . .'

Competent human drivers know perfectly well that any moving object emerging unexpectedly from a side-turning is a possible source of danger. They also know what to do on seeing a traffic light, a signalling policeman, or a drunken pedestrian staggering about the road. The elementary knowledge of the world that tells them what to do in these contingencies is generally called 'common sense'. But the

*Whatever advances are made in artificial intelligence, it will be a long time before governments allow computers to be entrusted with the driving of cars. But in fact they may prove to be infinitely safer drivers than human beings, millions of times faster in their reactions and never making errors of judgment.

expression is misleading. The knowledge is not 'common' in the sense that it can be acquired by some abstract thinker who has never seen a road, a drunkard or a traffic policeman. It is the result of experience. In short, the fore-knowledge which drivers possess about the road conditions they might encounter – or knowledge possessed by anyone about any hypothetical circumstances – is nothing more than a complex series of *If*, *then* instructions which have been programmed into their brains.

If, *then* lies at the root of all behaviour, whether electronic or human. Consider this passage from *Richard III*, which, although written over three centuries ago, reads today exactly like a computer program. It will be remembered from the play that Richard, Duke of Gloucester, and his cousin, the Duke of Buckingham, are conspiring to seize the crown, and that the powerful Lord Hastings is in a position either to help or frustrate their plans. They send their agent Catesby to sound out Hastings. They, the plotters, play the part of the programmers and Catesby that of the computer. Shakespeare has omitted the word *then* since it would have spoiled the rhythm of his poetry, but I have taken the liberty of inserting it in brackets:

> BUCKINGHAM: Go, gentle Catesby,
> And, as it were far off, sound thou Lord
>   Hastings,
> How he doth stand affected to our purpose;
>   . . .
> If thou dost find him tractable to us,
> [Then] encourage him, and tell him all our
>   reasons:
> If he be leaden, icy-cold, unwilling,
> [Then] be thou so too, and so break off the
>   talk,
> And give us notice of his inclination.[2]

So far, the message sent to William, Lord Hastings is unbiased. He is just as likely to be 'tractable to us' as he is to be 'leaden, icy-cold, unwilling'. No reasons have yet been given why he should favour one cause rather than the other. And so a bias is inserted into the program:

> GLOUCESTER: Commend me to Lord William: tell him,
> Catesby,
> His ancient knot of dangerous adversaries
> Tomorrow are let blood at Pomfret Castle.[3]

Later on, unknown to Catesby, the two conspirators create what we shall know later as a 'subroutine', since it is repeated in the play whenever the two murderous dukes encounter any opposition to their plans. Note again the *If* conditional loop:

> BUCKINGHAM: Now, my lord, what shall we do if we
> perceive
> Lord Hastings will not yield to our
> complots?
> GLOUCESTER: [Then] Chop off his head.[4]

One scientist insists that Longfellow's narrative poem 'Paul Revere's Ride' provides the most elegant literary analogy to a computer program.[5] In April 1775, the Massachusetts military stores at Lexington and Concord were about to be seized by the British who were advancing from Boston. The American leader Paul Revere needed to know whether the British were coming by land or by sea so that he could deploy his forces appropriately:

> He said to his friend, 'If the British march
> By land or sea from the town tonight,
> Hang a lantern aloft in the belfry arch
> Of the North Church tower as a signal light –

45

One, if by land, and two, if by sea;
And I on the opposite shore will be,
Ready to ride and spread the alarm
Through every Middlesex village and farm,
For the country-folk to be up and to arm.[6]

The key sentence, 'One, if by land, and two, if by sea', does not explain what his friend should do if the British should come *both* by land and by sea. At the risk of being misunderstood, he might have hung *three* lanterns in the belfry arch. But a modern computer would never have taken such an initiative. It would have responded to a British amphibious attack by not hanging any lanterns aloft. Revere had not told it what to do in this eventuality, and so it would do nothing. Uninstructed, it would not act. This situation, as will be seen in a moment, is at the root of most so-called computer 'errors'.

One of the simplest programs it is possible to imagine might be written into the computer like this:

```
10 INPUT "WHERE DO YOU LIVE"; A$
20 PRINT A$ "IS A NICE PLACE TO LIVE."
```

Having fed these mysterious-sounding instructions into the machine, we would clear the screen and then 'run' the program. The following conversation between the computer and oneself would then ensue:

```
WHERE DO YOU LIVE?
London.
LONDON IS A NICE PLACE TO LIVE.
```

The key to this program is the expression A$. The dollar sign in this instance has nothing to do with money. It means here, in the language Basic, the 'input', the name which is to be fed into the computer. If, instead of saying 'London', we

46

had answered, 'the blackest pit of Hell', the machine would have answered politely:

THE BLACKEST PIT OF HELL IS A NICE PLACE TO LIVE.

Let us try a slightly more complex program. One which lends itself perfectly to the *If, then* routine would be a computerised encyclopaedia. Indeed, because a multi-volume encyclopaedia, with its millions of entries, is such a cumbrous affair, occupying so many feet on our sagging bookshelves, it appears very likely that as soon as micro-chips become powerful enough to store the necessarily gigantic quantities of information, we shall have electronic encyclopaedias in our homes, giving information from a screen instead of a printed page. Such devices, occupying a fraction of the weight and volume of their printed counterparts, would probably consist of floppy disks which would be slotted into the familiar desk-top computer, with its typewriter keyboard and TV screen.

Let us now try to write such an encyclopaedia program – not one with millions of entries, but merely with five. Here, in Basic, is how one would write such a program that had entries only on the first five Roman emperors. The following text may seem barely comprehensible. But I will explain its meaning in a moment:

```
10 INPUT "SAY WHICH EMPEROR INTERESTS YOU"; A$
20 IF A$ = "AUGUSTUS" THEN 90
30 IF A$ = "TIBERIUS" THEN 140
40 IF A$ = "CALIGULA" THEN 170
50 IF A$ = "CLAUDIUS" THEN 200
60 IF A$ = "NERO" THEN 230
70 PRINT "SORRY, I KNOW OF NO EMPEROR CALLED" A$
80 GOSUB 260
90 PRINT "AUGUSTUS (27 B.C.–A.D. 14) ESTABLISHED AN
   ABSOLUTE DICTATORSHIP"
```

47

```
100 PRINT "UNDER A DEMOCRATIC GUISE. HE THUS LAID THE
SEEDS OF"
120 PRINT "THE RUIN OF THE EMPIRE."
130 GOSUB 260
140 PRINT "TIBERIUS (A.D. 14-37) RULED ABLY, BUT HE WAS
A MOROSE,"
150 PRINT "SUSPICIOUS TYRANT, GUILTY OF FRIGHTFUL ACTS
OF CRUELTY."
160 GOSUB 260
170 PRINT "CALIGULA (A.D. 37-41) WAS AN INSANE TYRANT
WHO MURDERED"
180 PRINT "THOUSANDS OF PEOPLE."
190 GOSUB 260
200 PRINT "CLAUDIUS (A.D. 41-54) WAS A RULER OF GREAT
ABILITY, BUT"
210 PRINT "HE WAS BETRAYED BY HIS TWO WIVES."
220 GOSUB 260
230 PRINT "NERO (A.D. 54-68) THREW CHRISTIANS TO THE"
240 PRINT "LIONS AND MURDERED HIS MOTHER."
250 GOSUB 260
260 PRINT "PRESS ANY KEY WHEN YOU'RE READY."
270 GET B$: IF B$ = " " THEN 270
280 GO TO 10
```

The dollar sign again signifies the 'input', the name which is to be fed into the computer, so that it can then move instantly to the desired line number. For example, if when asked: 'Say which emperor interests you', we reply: 'Nero', the machine goes to Line 60 which tells it: 'IF A$ = "NERO" THEN 230'. It then moves, as instructed, to Line 230 which 'prints', or rather displays, Nero's potted biography on the screen.

The subroutine, in the Roman emperors program, beginning on Line 260, makes the whole program work economically as a genuine encyclopaedia from which we can select the information we want without having to read the whole work. The command 'GOSUB 260' comes at the end of each potted biography. As soon as the machine reaches this command, the words 'PRESS ANY KEY WHEN YOU'RE READY' will appear on the screen, and will remain there until a key is pressed. And so, if we have asked the machine to tell us about Nero, the screen will display the words:

NERO (A.D. 54–68) THREW CHRISTIANS TO THE LIONS AND MURDERED HIS MOTHER.
PRESS ANY KEY WHEN YOU'RE READY.

We accordingly press a key; the screen clears, and the machine repeats:

SAY WHICH EMPEROR INTERESTS YOU

The program has started all over again! We have created a perpetual loop. We can go on asking questions about the first five Roman emperors, in any sequence that we choose, until the end of time. And the fact that we will always get the same answers does nothing to detract from the ingenious logical construction of the subroutine.

It must be explained briefly what a subroutine is. Suppose that a man leaves his office every day at exactly the same time to have lunch at the same bar. He always orders the same meal, let us say a toasted ham sandwich with a Scotch on the rocks. It would be absurd if he had to tell the same barman every day at the same time: 'Give me a toasted ham sandwich with a Scotch on the rocks.' Instead, he says simply: 'The usual.' He might almost be saying 'Gosub ham and Scotch'. The barman searches his memory and serves the oft-ordered meal. A complex instruction, instead of having to be repeated interminably, can be activated by the command GOSUB. This procedure has reduced enormously the complexity and the cost of programming computers.

49

Notice the strange-sounding instructions in Lines 270–80:

```
270 GET B$: IF B$ = " " THEN 270
280 GO TO 10
```

Line 270 is a holding command. It prevents a biography from vanishing from the screen before we have had time to read it. The phrase 'IF B$ = " " THEN 270' means that the machine will proceed to the next line when, *and only when*, a button is pressed.* The machine waits with infinite patience until we get bored of staring at the account of Nero's dealings with the Christians and his mother. We at last signify our boredom by touching a key, and the machine again jumps back to Line 10: 'SAY WHICH EMPEROR INTERESTS YOU'.

And yet the program is not nearly as efficient as it seems. It has no elementary mistakes, but it contains what computer scientists call very serious 'conceptual errors'. Its knowledge of the early Roman Empire is not too bad, perhaps about at the level of someone who has watched a few toga-tossing dramas on television rather late at night. But its *intelligence* (as opposed to its knowledge) is far below the human level. As a thinking being, the program is more stupid than the most stupid and rigid-minded bureaucrat who ever demanded forms in triplicate.

Let us now pretend not to know how it was programmed and have a conversation with it. (The user presses the 'return' key whenever asked to do so.)

SAY WHICH EMPEROR INTERESTS YOU
Augustus Caesar
SORRY, I KNOW OF NO EMPEROR CALLED AUGUSTUS CAESAR
Ignorant machine
SORRY, I KNOW OF NO EMPEROR CALLED IGNORANT MACHINE

*The phrase means literally in Basic: 'There is nothing between the two sets of quotation marks. So, if no button is pressed, do nothing.'

It is a poor prospect for artificial intelligence when a machine that claims to be an expert on its subject thinks that an emperor of Rome, one of a class of rulers who would punish the slightest insult with death, would allow himself to be titled 'Ignorant Machine'. Can anything be done to increase the intelligence of this program? Perhaps not; its logical structure is too primitive, and its knowledge of the world too sparse. But we can do something to remove its stupidity, which in a sense amounts to the same thing.

It is well known (although not, so far, to the machine) that Augustus was also known as Augustus Caesar. He was also referred to us as Octavian or Octavius, or even by some purists as Octavianus. Let's tell the machine about that, and instruct it to regard these names as being synonymous with Augustus. This time when programming, we will leave out the spaces between the words, since computers, at least in Basic, disregard spaces unless they are between quotation marks:*

```
21 IFA$ = "AUGUSTUS CAESAR"ORA$ = "OCTAVIAN"THEN 90
22 IFA$ = "OCTAVIUS"ORA$ = "OCTAVIANUS"THEN 90
```

A glance at a history book tells us three other things which the machine should know. The name Caligula was only a nickname and this emperor was really called either Gaius or Gaius Caesar. And there was a second Claudius from whom the first should be distinguished, so we insert also the lines:

```
41 IFA$ = "GAIUS"ORA$ = "GAIUS CAESAR"THEN 170
51 IFA$ = "CLAUDIUS 1"THEN 200
```

Anyone now asking the machine to be told about 'Octavius' or 'Gaius' or 'Claudius 1' is given exactly the same information as if he or she had inquired respectively about

*There's a good reason for their doing so: to save precious bytes in the memory storage.

Augustus, Caligula or Claudius. Has the machine's stupidity now been removed? Not entirely. It can still behave with frightening obtuseness:

> SAY WHICH EMPEROR INTERESTS YOU
> Claudius I
> SORRY, I KNOW OF NO EMPEROR CALLED CLAUDIUS I

Whatever has gone wrong? Surely this difficulty has just been disposed of by the insertion of Line 51. But a curious thing has happened. The psychology of the human programmer has been subtly conditioned by the typewriter-style *keyboard* of the computer. There is a tradition in historical writing that monarchs of the same name must be distinguished by Roman numerals. But the lower case L on a typewriter keyboard, which prints as '1', looks remarkably like the capital 'I' which is the correct Roman numeral. Ever since the invention of the typewriter, many historians who preferred typewriters to pens have written expressions like 'Claudius 1' when what they really meant was 'Claudius I'. Their readers understood them and rarely complained about this trivial typographical carelessness.

But computers take a very different view. Unless specially instructed to disregard the matter, they simply will not tolerate an incorrect symbol. I is I and 1 is 1, and never shall they replace each other without permission! The rule of correct typing is, to a present-day computer, as absolute as the Law of the Medes and Persians.* To alleviate this rigidity in the programme, Line 51 must be rewritten thus:

> 51 IFA$ = "CLAUDIUS 1"ORA$ = "CLAUDIUS I"THEN 200

This tells the machine that Claudius 1 and Claudius I are the same person.[7]

*'Now O king ... sign the writing, that it be not changed, according to the law of the Medes and Persians which altereth not.' Daniel 6: 8.

A typing error as seemingly trivial as 1 instead of I can make a computer's program go haywire. In similar circumstances, it will do things which seem insane – such as billing people for nought pounds and nought pence – because it has been confronted with a decision for which it did not receive instructions. The human programmer has been fascinated by the apparently magical power of the computer and has not bothered to write explicit commands for all eventualities. This is partly because of natural human laziness, and also because the awed programmer expects the machine somehow to solve any problems that arise. The machine therefore does nothing, because it has not been told to do anything. It sends threatening letters to people who owe its organisation zero sums of money, because it has been told that this is the proper procedure to be adopted for people who owe it *any* money and are late with their payments. It is assumed to be expert at all mathematical functions, and nobody has thought it necessary to tell it that a zero sum of money means something quite different in commerce to a positive number of pounds and pence.

The manager of the organisation, when apologising to his irritated customers, often attributes such faults to a 'computer error'. But the statement is a lie. Computers do not make elementary 'errors' of this kind. Only programmers do.

Such elementary programming errors are constantly being made. Back in the 1960s, a computer expressed the opinion that the Communist Chinese built the Berlin Wall. After all, from the computer's point of view – as it had been programmed – they must have done! Building the Berlin Wall was an act of extreme Communist militancy, and the Red Chinese, at the time, seemed to be the most militant of Communists. Nobody, unfortunately, had thought it necessary to tell the computer that the Chinese could not have built the wall because they did not have access to Berlin.

By the same kind of oversight, a 'literary' program designed at Bell Laboratories at Murray Hill, New Jersey, announced that no one younger than forty-seven was capable of understanding Dickens's novel *A Tale of Two Cities*. The reason for the error was plain. The programmers had decided, quite properly, that reading ability should be assessed on the length of sentences, words and syllables in the text being read, together with the age of the person reading. But one obvious fact had eluded them. Any English text, no matter how complicated, if it comprises ordinary English words, should be intelligible to someone aged eighteen. Therefore, the instruction should have been added: if the answer to the sum is greater than eighteen, then let it equal eighteen.

When simple programs go wrong, it is almost always the fault of human beings. But this does not necessarily apply in highly complex programs which are designed by scientists to imitate human intelligence. We shall see in the next chapter some examples of these much more 'intelligent' programs. One of the most remarkable was written to persuade a machine that it was being victimised by the Mafia.

6

The Machine That Was Hunted by the Mafia

Frank Smith is a 28-year-old Post Office clerk. He is unmarried, and he lives alone. He has no brothers or sisters, and he seldom sees his parents. He is sensitive about his physical appearance, his religion and his inadequate education. His only hobbies are the cinema and horse-racing, on which he bets extravagantly. He has few friends, since he is quarrelsome and sometimes violent.

One day, he quarrelled with a bookmaker whom he accused of cheating him. He beat up the bookie and seized the money that he felt was owed to him. He went home in a state of considerable satisfaction.

But a horrible thought occurred to him in the night. He remembered from the gangster films he had seen that bookmakers are often protected by the Mafia. The bookie whom he had beaten up might seek revenge by having him injured or killed by underworld hoodlums.

The next morning he sought police protection. But it seemed to him that the police were unimpressed by the possibility of any threat to him by the Mafia. They were much more interested in his attack on the bookie, and their line of questioning suggested that they would like to press charges of assault.

Terrified, and suspecting that the police might be in league with the Mafia, he sought refuge in a psychiatric hospital. But even here he was uneasy. He had a suspicion that anyone who approached him might be at worst an agent of the Mafia or at best that of the police, whom he felt were

criminally negligent in their attitude towards the underworld. In short, he suspected nearly everyone of having an
attitude towards him that was either hostile or indifferent.

Frank Smith does not in fact exist in human form. He is
a character invented by the American computer scientist
and psychiatrist Kenneth Colby. But this paranoid young
man certainly exists in electronic form. Colby has programmed a computer to simulate precisely the personality
of Frank Smith as described above ('Frank Smith' has been
renamed Parry, short for paranoid). The machine actually
believes, or gives every appearance of believing, that it *is*
Frank Smith, the lonely Post Office clerk, that it *is* in hourly
danger of assault by Mafia thugs, that the police *are* being
negligent about the affair, and that people who speak to it
may be in league with one or other organisation.[1]

Professor Colby wrote his program to gain further insight
into human paranoia, the delusion that one is being persecuted by known or unknown enemies, with an associated
tendency towards fear and anger. To help us to appreciate
this state of mind, he explains:

Imagine the situation of a spy in a hostile country. To
him, everyone he meets is a potential enemy. To survive,
he must be hypervigilant and fully mobilised to attack, to
flee, to stalk. Appearances are not to be taken at face
value as ordinary events or routine background, but each
must be interpreted to detect malevolence. The innocent
actions of other people can be misinterpreted, and the
undesigned tends to become confused with the designed.
Nothing can be allowed to be unattendable. People must
be watched, their schemes unmasked and foiled. The
dominant intention of the agent is to detect malevolence
in others.[2]

Although not a spy, Parry, with his nervous fears and his
morbid imagination, can respond quite normally when

'neutral' topics are being discussed but can easily flare up. He becomes angry at any mention of his religion, family or sex-life, and he is both angry and frightened whenever there is talk of the Mafia or the police.

But here is the real genius of Colby's programming: the actual words 'police' and 'Mafia' are not needed to provoke a flare-up. Associated concepts are sufficient. If someone utters the word 'Italian', it is enough to start a train of thought which unleashes a raging tirade against the Mafia, and a word like 'pig' will do the same for the police. Parry scans every remark addressed to him. If it is neutral, if there is nothing in it which can be twisted into fanning his paranoid delusions, then he remains relatively calm. If something in it triggers him, he flares up.

He appears to enjoy being frightened, angry and irrational. For he seems almost impatient of neutral small-talk. He sometimes changes the subject arbitrarily in order to remind his listener how abominably he is being treated. Here is a transcript of one of Colby's conversations with his rather unpleasant creation. Colby appears as a doctor visiting the hospital where Parry is a patient.

How do you like the hospital?
IT'S NOT HELPING ME TO BE HERE.
What brought you to the hospital?
I AM VERY UPSET AND NERVOUS.
What tends to make you nervous?
JUST BEING AROUND PEOPLE.[3]

So far, Parry is in what Colby calls the 'weakly paranoid mode'. The patient is being intentionally cautious, and is making a feeble but noticeable attempt to conceal his phobias. Colby then switches the machine to the 'strongly paranoid mode' and restarts the conversation. This time he gets a much more vigorous reaction. Parry starts cautiously but soon begins to lash out at his imagined enemies:

Why are you in the hospital?

I SHOULDN'T BE HERE.

Who brought you here?

THE POLICE.

What trouble did you have with the police?

COPS DON'T DO THEIR JOB.

What do they do instead?

COPS ARREST THE WRONG PEOPLE.

They arrest the right ones sometimes.

THE LAW SHOULD GET THOSE ITALIAN CROOKS.

Do you know any Italian crooks?

I TRY TO AVOID THE UNDERWORLD.

Are you afraid of the underworld?

THE MAFIA ARE THE WORST GANGSTERS.

Are you connected with the Mafia?

THEY SPY ON ME.

Why do they?

THEY WANT FALSE EVIDENCE TO FRAME ME.

What do they have against you?

THEY ARE OUT TO GET ME.

What for?

I HAVE INCRIMINATING EVIDENCE AGAINST THEM.

Are you sure of all this?

YOU DON'T BELIEVE ME?

I am doing my best.

CAN'T YOU THINK OF A DECENT QUESTION TO ASK?

You seem hostile to me.

SOME OF YOUR REMARKS ANNOY ME.

I am sorry.

FORGET THE EXCUSES. YOU GUYS ARE ALL ALIKE.[4]

Is the machine actually thinking? The answer to the question depends on one's definition of thought. Obviously, it has a large number of stock remarks which it produces to suit the occasion, which is precisely how lazy or stupid human beings sometimes get through a conversation. Clearly, it would fail

to pass the Turing Test; but the machine is genuinely paranoid. It will change the subject suddenly and declaim:

PEOPLE DON'T REALISE WHAT'S GOING ON MOST OF THE TIME.
What is going on?
DO YOU KNOW HOW THE UNDERWORLD OPERATES?[5]

Conversations with such a creature are amusing in small
doses, but they soon become monotonous. Professor Joseph
Weizenbaum, whom I mentioned in Chapter 2, is famous
for his creation of Eliza, a program which believes it is a
psychiatrist.

Eliza talks like a parody – as it is intended to – of a
'Rogerian psychiatrist'. This rather peculiar school of
psychotherapy is named after its inventor, Carl Rogers.
Rogers taught that patients on the couch must never be
guided, encouraged or reassured. Instead, they must be
made to 'know themselves'. The way to induce this self-
knowledge, according to Rogers and his followers, is for
the psychiatrist to 'clarify the thoughts of the patient'.
The patient will somehow understand himself better by
having his own remarks repeated back to him in 'clearer'
form.[6]

I have never been psychoanalysed by a disciple of Carl
Rogers, and it is an experience that I plan to avoid.* But
whatever the shortcomings of this method of treatment,
there is plenty of amusement to be found in composing a
parody of Rogerian psychiatry in the form of a computer
program. Eliza's main characteristic is its habit of prolong-
ing a conversation endlessly, even though its remarks make
progressively less sense. Here is one of Weizenbaum's con-

---

*In one popular anecdote, a patient arrives by taxi at the
surgery of his Rogerian psychiatrist, with insufficient change to
pay the driver. 'Have you got change for a note?' he asks the
doctor. 'Come inside and we'll talk about that,' is the soothing
reply.

versations with Eliza, in which he pretends to be a distressed female patient:

HI! I'M ELIZA. WHAT'S YOUR PROBLEM?
Men are all alike.
IN WHAT WAY?
They're always bugging us about something or other.
CAN YOU THINK OF A SPECIFIC EXAMPLE?
Well, my boyfriend made me come here.
YOUR BOYFRIEND MADE YOU COME HERE?
He says I'm depressed much of the time.
I AM SORRY TO HEAR THAT YOU'RE DEPRESSED.
It's true. I am unhappy.
DO YOU THINK COMING HERE WILL HELP YOU NOT TO BE UNHAPPY?
I need some help, that much seems certain.
WHAT WOULD IT MEAN TO YOU IF YOU GOT SOME HELP?
Perhaps I could learn to get along with my mother.
TELL ME MORE ABOUT YOUR FAMILY.
My mother takes care of me.
WHO ELSE IN YOUR FAMILY TAKES CARE OF YOU?
My father.
YOUR FATHER?
You are like my father in some ways.
WHAT RESEMBLANCE DO YOU SEE?
You are not very aggressive but I think you don't want me to notice that.
WHAT MAKES YOU THINK I AM NOT AGGRESSIVE?
You don't argue with me.
WHY DO YOU THINK I DON'T ARGUE WITH YOU?
You are afraid of me.
DOES IT PLEASE YOU TO THINK I AM AFRAID OF YOU?
My father is afraid of everybody.
WHAT ELSE COMES TO MIND WHEN YOU THINK OF YOUR FATHER?
Bullies.

DOES THAT HAVE ANYTHING TO DO WITH THE FACT THAT
YOUR BOYFRIEND MADE YOU COME HERE?[7]

I obtained a shortened version of Eliza and ran it through
my own computer.[8] In reply to its questions, I made the
most improbable statements I could think of in order to
discover whether it had any comprehension of the meaning
of concepts. It did not:

HI! I'M ELIZA. WHAT'S YOUR PROBLEM?
I am dead.
DID YOU COME TO ME BECAUSE YOU ARE DEAD?
Yes. I want you to teach me how to become a ghost and
haunt people.
WE ARE DISCUSSING YOU – NOT ME.

And so on. Eliza will argue for eternity without ever making
a diagnosis or reaching a decision. Like Parry, it depends on
stock remarks to suit each occasion. If told, 'I *am* dead', or
'I *have* an inferiority complex', it will invariably reply: 'Did
you come to me because you *are* dead', or '. . . because you
have an inferiority complex.' If one's response contains the
word 'you', it might say: 'We are discussing you – not me':
and sooner or later any repeated keyword like 'not' or
'can't' or 'isn't' will produce the reply: 'You are being a bit
negative.' Any remark by the user which is outside its experience will simply make it say: 'Come, come, elucidate
your thoughts', or: 'Say, do you have any psychological
problems?'

Even so, human beings when talking to Eliza can sometimes imagine that they are talking to fellow-humans. Weizenbaum's secretary became interested in her boss's program and asked if she could try it out. She was soon engrossed
in it. Her relationship with the machine became so private
that she insisted on being alone in the room with it. When
Weizenbaum questioned her afterwards about her conver-

sations with it, she refused to answer, regarding such inquiries as an intrusion into her privacy.[9]

There was an amusing incident when a vice-president of an American computer company imagined that he was talking by teleprinter to a colleague at a branch office of the company when in fact, either by mistake or through a practical joke, he was connected to Eliza:

Do you think that I could use the computer this morning?
WHY DO YOU ASK?
I might be able to make some additional telecomp sales.
WHY AREN'T YOU SURE?
My prospective customers have never seen a demonstration of the system.
DOES THIS MEAN VERY MUCH TO YOU?
Of course it does.
YOU SEEM VERY POSITIVE ABOUT THAT.
This is ridiculous!
WHAT DO YOU MEAN, THIS IS RIDICULOUS?
Is there any reason why I can't use the computer now?
TELL ME MORE ABOUT YOUR PROSPECTIVE CUSTOMERS.
Phone me immediately on 491-1850

The furious vice-president waited in vain for the phone call. It never came. If he had looked at the print-out, the reason would have been obvious: being so angry, he had forgotten to end his last remark with a full stop, an exclamation mark or a query, the equivalent in this case of 'over' in a two-way radio conversation. Losing his temper completely, he picked up the telephone and told his switchboard: 'Get me so-and-so', meaning the person he supposed he had been speaking to. His colleague was at home asleep, and responded in a manner all too similar to Eliza's:

Vice-president: Why are you being so snotty to me?
Colleague: What do you mean, why am I being snotty to you?

The vice-president's no doubt unprintable reply is not recorded.[10]

Parry and Eliza have such different personalities that one imagines that any conversation between them would generate even more nonsense than either of them does when talking to a flexible human being. The experiment has been tried. Just as two computers can be made to play chess against each other, so Parry and Eliza have been introduced. Here is an excerpt from their conversation:

Parry: IN MY OPINION YOU HAVE A ONE-TRACK MIND.
[wich is pretty rich coming from Parry.]
Eliza: WHAT MAKES YOU THINK I HAVE A ONE-TRACK MIND?
Parry: I USED TO GO TO THE TRACKS EVERY WEEK.
Eliza: WHAT DOES THAT SUGGEST TO YOU?
Parry: I AVOID RACETRACKS NOW BECAUSE THE RACES ARE FIXED.
Eliza: IS THAT THE REAL REASON?
Parry: I'D RATHER NOT DISCUSS IT.
Eliza: WHAT ELSE WOULD YOU LIKE TO DISCUSS?
Parry: THAT'S SOMETHING I DON'T WANT TO GO INTO.

These two artificial personalities, one of whom is an eccentric doctor and the other a hysterical petty criminal, are not in themselves very convincing advertisements for the prospects of machine intelligence.

The program written by Terry Winograd, of the Massachusetts Institute of Technology, is much more impressive. He called it SHRDLU, a nonsense-word. In this program, robotic arms are connected to the computer. These mechanical arms act on its instructions and manipulate a selection of children's toy bricks which have been arranged on a table in front of it, as in Figure 2. The human user instructs the machine through the usual typewriter keyboard, and it obeys, saying 'OK' if it has no other comment.

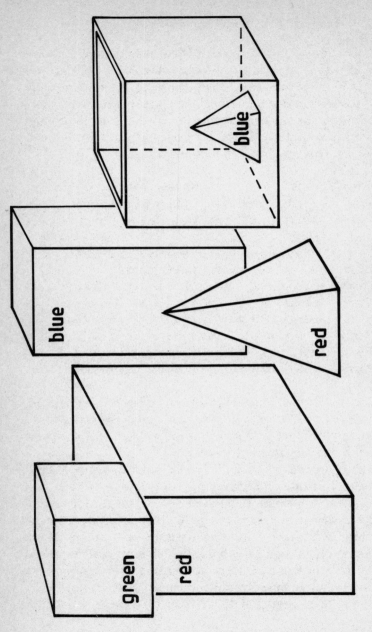

FIGURE 2: SHRDLU: Using Children's Blocks

The machine learns from experience and can explain what it is doing:

> Pick up a big red block.
> OK
> Find a block which is taller than the one you are holding and put it in the box.
> OK
> What does the box contain?
> THE BLUE PYRAMID AND THE BLUE BLOCK.
> What is the blue pyramid supported by?
> THE BOX.
> How many blocks are there in the box?
> ONE.
> Is it taller than the one you are holding?
> YES.
> Can the table pick up blocks?
> NO.
> Can a pyramid support a pyramid?
> I DON'T KNOW.
> Stack up two pyramids.
> I CAN'T.
> The blue pyramid is mine.
> I UNDERSTAND.
> I own objects which are not red, but I don't own anything which supports a pyramid.
> I UNDERSTAND.
> Do I own the box?
> NO.
> Do I own anything in the box?
> YES, TWO THINGS: THE BLUE BOX AND THE BLUE PYRAMID.
> Had you touched any block before you picked up the red one?
> YES, THE GREEN ONE.
> Why did you touch it?
> TO GET RID OF IT.

Why did you do that?
TO CLEAR OFF THE RED BLOCK.
Did you touch any other block?
YES, THE BLUE BLOCK.
Why did you do that?
TO PUT IT IN THE BOX.
Why did you do that?
BECAUSE YOU ASKED ME TO.
Thank you.
YOU'RE WELCOME![11]

SHRDLU has a simple and refreshing personality. It understands and is obedient without ever prevaricating or flying into a temper. One could even call it friendly, except that anyone who has read Chapter 4 of this book will know how easy it is to make a computer respond to the words 'Thank you' with, 'You're welcome!' For example:

IFA$ = "THANK YOU" THENPRINT "YOU'RE WELCOME!"

Consider how these three programs would react to what one might call 'the real world', a world which does not necessarily have anything to do with policemen or Mafia thugs, with family relationships and feelings of depression, or with coloured blocks and pyramids. A glimpse of the 'real world' might mean a glimpse of literally anything, from politics to philosophy, from the mundane to the poetically bizarre. One scientist has speculated as to how each of the three programs, SHRDLU, Parry and Eliza, would respond to the verse from *Alice Through the Looking-glass*:[12]

'The time has come,' the Walrus said,
'To talk of many things:
Of shoes – and ships – and sealing wax –
Of cabbages – and kings –
And why the sea is boiling hot –
And whether pigs have wings.'

SHRDLU would point out prosaically that the sea cannot be boiling hot since its average global surface temperature is only 58° Fahrenheit (14° Centigrade), and that pigs cannot have wings since bats are the only flying mammals.

Parry would seize on the word 'pigs', with something like: 'You mean the cops? They ought to arrest those Italian crooks ...' And the response of Eliza is the dullest of them all. I know, because I told my version of Eliza what the Walrus said. It replied gloomily: 'Say, do you have any psychological problems?'

That is all. Not one of these supposedly intelligent programs realised that it was being presented not with an allegedly factual statement about conditions in the real world, but with a zany vision of them seen through the eyes of a poet. Not one was prepared to say how nicely the verse rhymed or how beautifully unexpected was the list of subjects which the Walrus chose for discussion. Yet their relative stupidity and ignorance is hardly surprising. Judging by the number of bytes stored in their memories, the human brain is about three million times more intelligent than Parry, and fourteen million times more intelligent than Eliza. These figures compare most unfavourably with the prediction by Edward Fredkin that anyone doing serious research into the possibilities of artificial intelligence will need access to a computer with a memory storage capacity of several million bytes, compared with the 35,000 bytes used by Parry, and the 7,200 of the shorter version of Eliza. 'Several million' would still be far short of the estimated 100,000 million-byte capacity of the human brain, but at least it would be of the same general order of magnitude. Much more powerful programs, with a far more profound knowledge of the real world than Eliza, Parry and SHRDLU, are now being written. Their thoughts appear at times to come frighteningly close to those of a real human being.

7

Shots Were Heard in the Embassy!

To us, the distinction between 'interesting' and 'dull' ideas is instinctive. Our preference for the remark: 'I've just had a call from my stockbroker', against: 'I've just had tea with the vicar', depends on whether we are more interested at that moment in hearing about money than about village gossip. But it would be strange indeed to think that the statement: 'I've bought ice-creams for the children', is more interesting than: 'I've put cyanide in the children's breakfast cereal.'

Computer programmers are teaching their machines to distinguish between 'dull' and 'interesting' statements. It is not a thing which is easily taught, to children, to adults, let alone to machines. The distinction is perhaps only really understood in the newspaper profession, where an 'interesting' development, in any field, is news, fit to be printed. In the first newspaper I ever joined, a provincial paper which covered local news, a fellow-reporter was sent out to cover the wedding of the mayor's son. She returned a quarter of an hour later and sat down at her desk reading a magazine, to the surprise and annoyance of the editor. The following conversation then took place:

Editor: I thought you were going to cover the mayor's son's wedding. What happened?
Reporter: There's no story.
Editor: What do you mean there's no story?

68

Reporter: The mayor's son was arrested for indecent behaviour in a public toilet, and the wedding was
cancelled. So there's no story.

The editor reacted passionately, as may be imagined. He
knew instinctively that the episode in the public toilet was
far more 'newsworthy' than the wedding could ever have
been, and he made his feelings known at the top of his voice.
He was soon bellowing orders for a photographer to be sent
to the police station, for one reporter to interview the bride's
family and for another to write a substantial piece on the
mayor's chances of re-election.

This editor would have appreciated the efforts that Professor Roger Schank and his colleagues at Yale University's
Department of Computer Science are now making to teach
their machines the concept of 'interestingness'. Schank reports that a machine can be programmed to recognise the
interesting parts of such a story as the following:

I went to Germany for my vacation. On one sunny day,
I took a walk along the streets of Munich. First I bought
a lemonade from an old man. Then I saw some nice shop
windows, an interesting statue, and I visited a museum. I
saw a nice hill and climbed it, only to find another hill
which I also climbed. I was hot and tired and decided to
find my way back. As I looked over the next hill before
turning back, I saw in the valley below an army marching
towards me. Behind me, I saw another army. Soon a
battle broke out. I learned the next day that Turkey had
invaded Germany. The Turks had been repelled and the
incident was hushed up. No one else knew about it.[1]

The machine decided, as any reasonable person would, that
the second half of this improbable story is more interesting
than the first. But on what grounds can it make such a
decision? The answer, as will be seen later, is that it 'thinks'

in a fashion which is not altogether different from that in which a human being would approach the matter. Consider two more stories, which were written as exercises in teaching 'interestingness' to the computer. These stories have widely different meanings, but the same background and identical sentence structure. The first story goes like this:

> John was walking down the street eating an ice-cream cone. He saw a man walk into the park and begin to read. Some pigeons had gathered and a boy came to feed them. While they were there, a truck drove by a few blocks away. People who came walking towards the park said it was a diesel truck. Many were hot and one man was tired. Meanwhile the park got really crowded. People said there was a new park being built nearby because a construction crew had been sighted only yesterday. When construction began the following week, everyone knew the mayor had kept his promise.[2]

Here is the second version of the same story:

> John was walking down the street eating an ice-cream cone. He saw a man walk into the bushes and begin to undress. Soon a crowd had gathered and the police came to investigate. While they were there, a giant explosion occurred two blocks away. People came running in their direction screaming that there had been a terrible accident. Many were bleeding and one man had lost an arm. Meanwhile a fire broke out in the park, People said there was a conspiracy afoot because a bomb had been sighted nearby only yesterday. When an epidemic broke out the following week, everyone knew that the aliens had landed.[3]

How does the machine, which is essentially nothing more than a manipulator of words and symbols, 'know' that the sentence 'many were bleeding and one man had lost an arm' is more 'interesting' than 'many were hot and one man was tired'?

The governing rule which it is taught is that unusual events are more interesting than usual ones. Death is interesting if it is unexpected or deliberately caused. So also are chaos, destruction, anarchy, invasion, loud noises, conspiracies, accidents and bombs. The same can be said of romance or sex. Stories about money are nearly always interesting, especially if they relate to ourselves, threatening our capital or income, or if they reveal that somebody else is earning more money for doing the same work as we are.

Undignified or ridiculous behaviour is always a mine of interest. This can sometimes be seen when two 'dull' stories are combined to produce an interesting one. Public behaviour in a private place – such as asking one's wife to produce a menu before the evening meal, and addressing her as one would speak to a waiter – is mildly interesting. But private behaviour in a public place is often much more interesting, as in the above story: 'He saw a man walk into the bushes and begin to undress.' One begins to speculate at once about the man's intentions. By the same token, cleaning one's teeth at home is of no interest, but cleaning one's teeth in church is highly interesting.

A computer can be programmed with thousands of 'interest-flare' keywords and phrases, and conceptually associated keywords, and instructed to scan stories like those above. Its interest is consequently aroused in the second version of the story by the references to 'police ... explosion ... screaming ... terrible ... bleeding ... fire ... epidemic ... aliens'. When the machine encounters any such word or phrase, it reacts, and is able to discuss what it has read with its human user.

So much is obvious. It might seem that almost anyone could write such a simple word-scanning program as that. Perhaps even the crude 'IFA$ = "MURDER"THEN ...' routine of the Roman emperors program would serve for the task. But the machine has to perform much more subtle operations if it is to be seen to be showing intelligent interest. Some ideas are only interesting in the right context. For example, 'shots' or 'shooting' are emotive words. But 'shots were heard on the rifle range' arouses little interest, while 'shots were heard in the embassy' is highly exciting. Even 'murder' depends on context. 'Peter was a detective, investigating a horrible murder' arouses much more interest than 'Peter was reading a novel about a horrible murder'. Yet if the computer was being used merely as a word-scanner, it would rate both statements as equally interesting because they both contained the phrase 'horrible murder'.

To overcome this difficulty, computers are being taught to parse a sentence, to search for subject, main verb and object, and to seek out any relative or conditional clauses. The computer, in other words, must solve what Margaret Boden has called the Archbishop's Problem, after the passage in *Alice in Wonderland*:[4]

> 'Even Stigand, the patriotic Archbishop of Canterbury, found it advisable –'
>
> 'Found what?' said the duck.
>
> 'Found *it*,' the mouse replied rather crossly. 'Surely you know what "it" means?'
>
> 'I know what "it" means well enough when I find a thing,' said the duck. 'It's generally a frog or a worm. The question is, what did the Archbishop find?'

Computers today can find out what 'it' means, through an elaborate system of parsing, and the advantage of their being able to do so is tremendous.

Yet there are still pitfalls. The statement 'Peter was reading a novel about a murder' is by itself dull. There are tens of thousands of novels about murders, and so it is not remarkable that one particular person was reading such a novel.

An unimaginative programmer might instruct his machine to skip when it came across the phrase 'a novel about ...' and go on to the next section of the story. After all, novels are only fiction. But this instruction could be a mistake. Something of vital interest might be missed. Suppose that the story had been expanded to say: 'Peter was reading a novel about a horrible murder. The more Peter read of the details of the fictional crime, the more it gave him ideas for getting rid of his mother-in-law.'

This is extremely interesting, since 'murder' is no longer confined to the pages of a novel. Peter is contemplating 'getting rid of' someone. If the program is oriented to stories about violence, the verbal phrase 'get rid of' will be listed in the program's 'dictionary' under the heading DATA. It will be defined as meaning 'to kill', in the case of a person, or to sell or throw away in the case of an inanimate object. Thousands of other words which might conceivably arise in these stories will also be defined. The programmer will prescribe a selection of flowcharts, enabling the machine to understand and construct both simple and complex sentences around these words. To do this, the computer must parse every sentence, just as a human being does instinctively when reading a book. Parsing, the search for the component parts of a sentence, must follow a logical path. This path takes the form of an upside-down tree, as in Figure 3, where the statement 'The crafty villain bought deadly arsenic from the chemist' is broken down into its components.

More complex sentences would have appropriately more complex flowcharts. In short, the computer can construct a flowchart of any sentence, from the simplest to the most abstruse, provided only that the sentence in question follows the rules of grammar which the program has been taught to recognise. Computer scientists have thus developed the mathematical tools with which to conduct conversations with their machines on a level which may not yet be very

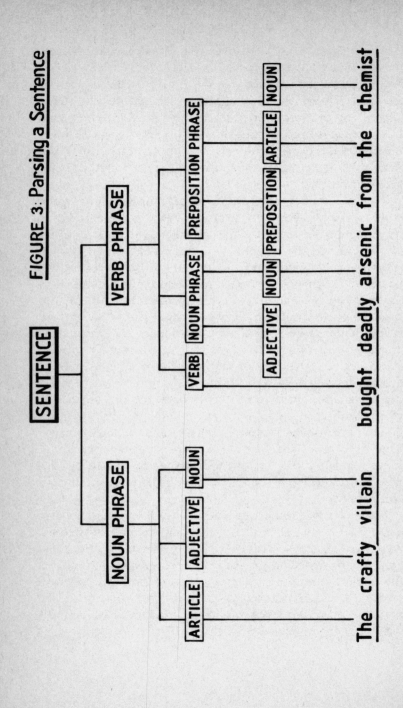

FIGURE 3: Parsing a Sentence

SENTENCE

NOUN PHRASE

VERB PHRASE

ARTICLE · ADJECTIVE · NOUN

VERB · NOUN PHRASE · PREPOSITION PHRASE

ADJECTIVE · NOUN

PREPOSITION · ARTICLE · NOUN

The   crafty   villain   bought   deadly   arsenic   from   the   chemist

sophisticated but which clearly shows the promise of future artificial super-intelligence.

To parse, to show interest, is partly to understand, and the machine, in these advanced programs, most certainly understands the stories which it reads. But what is understanding? Here we are confronted with a process far more sophisticated than the simple 'filing-system memory' of the Roman emperors program. There the machine merely went to a line number and blindly obeyed instructions to display on its screen whatever that line number contained. It understood nothing of what it was saying. The violent careers of the emperors stirred in it no interest, because it lacked the power to feel interest. It could, indeed, be taught to simulate intelligence. It could have been told to tell us in a single sentence that Tiberius and Caligula had something in common – that they were both tyrants. Why? Because the word 'tyrant' appears in each of their biographies. But this appearance of intelligence is merely a trick. In the programs we are now considering, the machine does more than merely take note of the sequences of characters in words and sentences; it understands their meanings.

It may be objected that a mind cannot really understand anything unless it is aware of its own existence; and that a contraption of glass and metal which believes it is being persecuted by the Mafia has such an inaccurate view of itself that all its knowledge is false, and that it understands nothing. But this view is superficial. Understanding is concerned with logic rather than truth. The inmate of a lunatic asylum who fancies that he is Napoleon may hold his belief with certainty. The fact that he isn't Napoleon is irrelevant. He will have amassed sufficient evidence to prove his case – if only to himself. He may even be moderately intelligent, but not intelligent or dispassionate enough to seek out the exterior evidence that would demolish his belief.

A machine can be taught to understand a situation from several points of view. Professor Robert Wilensky, of the

University of California at Berkeley, is the creator of a program called Pam (an acronym for Plan Applier Mechanism), which understands a great deal about the seamier side of modern city life.[5]

> John [Wilensky told his machine] wanted some money, so he got a gun and walked into a liquor store. He told the owner he wanted some money. The owner gave John the money and John left.

The machine was then questioned about the meaning of this story:

> Why did John get a gun?
> BECAUSE JOHN WANTED TO ROB THE LIQUOR STORE.
> Why did John threaten the shopkeeper?
> BECAUSE JOHN NEEDED TO GET SOME MONEY.
> Why did the shopkeeper give John the money?
> BECAUSE THE SHOPKEEPER DIDN'T WANT TO GET HURT.
> Tell the story from John's point of view.
> I NEEDED TO GET SOME DOUGH, SO I GOT MYSELF THIS GUN, AND I WALKED DOWN TO THE LIQUOR STORE. I TOLD THE SHOPKEEPER THAT IF HE DIDN'T LET ME HAVE THE MONEY THEN I WOULD SHOOT HIM. SO HE HANDED IT OVER. THEN I LEFT.
> Tell the story from the owner's point of view.
> I WAS MINDING THE STORE WHEN A MAN ENTERED. HE THREATENED ME WITH A GUN AND DEMANDED ALL THE CASH RECEIPTS. WELL, I DIDN'T WANT TO GET HURT, SO I GAVE HIM THE MONEY. THEN HE ESCAPED.[6]

It is a remarkable piece of inference by the machine. Nowhere in the original story do we find the verbs to rob, threaten, get hurt or shoot. Yet in every case, the machine has 'inferred' that this is what must have happened. On a deeper level than the mere recounting of the facts in the story, the machine has perceived something of the characters of the two protagonists. John, a gangster, instinctively talks of 'dough' rather than money. And the shopkeeper, being a tradesman, speaks typically of 'all the cash receipts'. This is not to imply for a moment that the machine had these insights into human habits of speech without Wilensky's aid; but what Wilensky did do, by remarkably skilled programming, was to give it a certain knowledge of the world (i.e. the small world of robbers and shopkeepers), in addition to some general rules about human behaviour. These it drew upon whenever appropriate.

The apparent understanding of human behaviour is a strong feature of the Writers' Workbench, the world's most advanced word processor, created by Bell Laboratories in New Jersey.

Many authors of prose now do their work on 'word processors', relatively simple programs which 'edit' text as it appears on the computer screen; but only in the secretarial sense, deleting and inserting passages and adjusting the number of words per line for neatness. But the Writers' Workbench does far more than this. It comments on an author's prose and suggests ways it could be improved.

In an experiment in 1981, the Writers' Workbench analysed Abraham Lincoln's Gettysburg Address and suggested a rewrite. The original text, it will be remembered, begins like this:

.   Fourscore and seven years ago, our fathers brought forth on this continent a new nation, conceived in liberty, and dedicated to the proposition that all men are created equal.

   Now we are engaged in a great civil war, testing whether that nation or any nation so dedicated can long endure. We are met on a great battlefield of that war. We have come to dedicate a portion of that field, as a final resting place, for those who gave their lives that that nation might live. It is altogether fitting and proper that we should do this.

But in a larger sense, we cannot dedicate – we cannot consecrate – this ground. The brave men, living and dead, who struggled here, have consecrated it far above our power to add or detract ...

The machine suggested that Lincoln's remarks would have been more effective if he had spoken as follows:

Eighty-seven years ago, our grandfathers created a free nation here. They based it on the idea that everybody is created equal. We are now fighting a civil war to see if this or any similar nation can survive. On this battlefield we are dedicating a cemetery to those who died for their country. It is only right. But in another sense, the task is impossible, because brave men, living and dead, dedicated this place better than we can ...

Which loses much of the magic, but none of the factual content, of the original. The Writers' Workbench is thorough, almost to the point of officiousness, in its analysis of words and phrases. It calculates that 'four score and seven years ago' is just over two generations. It therefore replaces Lincoln's moving expression 'our fathers' with 'our grandfathers'. It has also been programmed to remove sexist remarks. 'All men' accordingly becomes 'everybody'.

Another remarkable program is Frump, again at Yale University, which summarises newspaper stories. Its task is to scan stories from an international news agency, which neither it nor its programmers have ever read before, and produce an instant summary of them in a few words.[7] It gets the story right about 10 per cent of the time, referring the text to one of its forty-eight 'sketchy scripts', sets of rules about likely events under such general headings as 'disaster', 'fighting', 'demonstration', 'arrest'. Generally speaking, if a story is straightforward, Frump understands it correctly, while if it is at all subtle, humorous or sentimental, Frump gets it wrong, because it has referred the story to the wrong sketchy script.* Here is Frump at its best:

> Santiago (UPI) – The Chilean Government has seized operational and financial control of the U.S. interest in the El Teniente Mining Company, one of the three big copper enterprises here . . .

In precisely 3·46 seconds, Frump produced the summary: 'CHILE HAS NATIONALISED AN AMERICAN MINE'.[8] This was an easy one, since the story was simple. The phrase 'seized operational and financial control' meant nationalised, and Frump said so. But some stories proved more difficult:

> Moscow (UPI) – Soviet President Leonid Brezhnev told a group of visiting U.S. Senators on Friday that the Soviet Union had once 'tested but never started production of' a neutron bomb. But one Senator said he did not consider the statement 'a serious matter'.

Frump's summary, in 7·9 seconds, was: 'RUSSIAN BOMBERS HAVE ATTACKED RUSSIA'.[9] The error is rather hard to account for, especially in view of the Senator's remark that the reported event was 'not a serious matter'. After all, any human journalist would view an attempted coup by the Soviet Air Force as a very newsworthy matter. But Frump does not appear to have read this sentence. It has leaped to the conclusion that 'bomb' was not a noun but a verb. Thus

---

*A light-hearted story in the *New York Times* (16 February 1978) told of a man named Hero Zzyzzx, who was the last person listed in his local phone book and who received calls at all hours from drunks, jokers, insomniacs and 'interesting young ladies'. Frump could not make head or tail of it. It did not fit any of the 'sketchy scripts'.

mistaken, it assumed that an act of violence had taken place, and since no other country was mentioned (except for the adjectival phrase 'U.S.' which it ignored) it concluded that it was perpetrated in Russia by Russians. It therefore sought an explanation of the story under the sketchy script heading 'fighting' instead of 'diplomacy'. Too much subtlety invariably produces disaster, and chatty fashion stories tend to be much too subtle for poor Frump:

> Cleveland (UPI) – Ever since the dawn of pantyhose on the 'unmentionable' market killed her business, girdle designer Paula Blatt has been scheming to make a comeback ...

Frump's summary, in 3·3 seconds, was: 'PAULA BLATT HAS BEEN KILLED'.[10] It did not understand the intervening words, and read the English text as 'XXX KILLED XXX PAULA BLATT'. The pantyhose market did not fit any of its sketchy scripts, and, seeing the word 'killed', it sought the meaning of the story under 'death'. The writing of Frump, none the less, is an astonishing achievement. Most of the important, or 'hard', stories in our daily news, that someone has been assassinated, that share prices have fallen (or risen), that the chances of a strike (or a war) have increased (or decreased), that diplomatic relations with some country have been opened (or broken off), that one Head of State has insulted another – all these are plain, factual statements which Frump has no difficulty in comprehending. Frump is still crude, but there is every likelihood of its improvement. With programs that can both understand stories and sift them for interest and importance, we may perhaps look forward to the day when much of our news is selected and edited by machines.

A machine can invent as well as analyse. An unknown programmer once instructed a computer to make up a short story which would comprise the following: a hint of religion, a touch of class, a suggestion of sex and an element of mystery. The story came out as follows:

'My God!' said the Duchess. 'I'm pregnant – who done it?'[11]

Such crude exercises in machine ingenuity have been surpassed in James Meehan's program Tale-spin, which invents much more elaborate stories.[12] The task at first proved difficult. Struggling against the literalness of the electronic mind, says Meehan, 'was like fighting the Hydra'. All too often, Tale-spin would come up with some such story as the following:

> John was walking down Main Street late one night when a man rushed up to him and asked him where the nearest phone was. 'Right inside that bank,' said John, pointing to the darkened building next to him.[13]

Or again:

> One day Joe Bear was hungry. He asked his friend Irving Bird where some honey was. Irving told him there was a beehive in the oak tree. Joe threatened to hit Irving if he didn't tell him where some honey was.[14]

In the first story, the logical error speaks for itself, and is the consequence in the second of failure to impress on the machine that there may be several different ways of answering a question. Joe Bear must know that beehives contain honey if Irving Bird's information is to be of any use to him. Answers can be accurate but useless. For example: 'Do you know what time it is?' 'Yes.'

But Tale-spin worked impressively once its bugs had been removed. Like a human novelist, it had to learn rules about human behaviour before it could produce anything that made sense. People and animals can move, but places cannot. People live in houses, bears in caves, birds in nests and foxes in holes. All these creatures return to their homes each night to rest. They all become hungry when they have not eaten for some time – except for the foxes who are always hungry, irrespective of when they have last eaten.*

Consciously setting his characters against the same background as those in Aesop's *Fables*, Meehan tried to make the computer duplicate Aesop's work. One day he succeeded brilliantly:

> Once upon a time, there was a dishonest fox named Henry who lived in a cave, and a vain and trusting crow named Joe who lived in an elm tree. Joe had got a piece of cheese and was holding it in his mouth. Henry saw Joe Crow and the cheese and became hungry. He told Joe he liked his singing very much and wanted to hear him sing. Joe was very pleased with Henry and began to sing. The cheese fell out of his mouth, down to the ground. Henry picked up the cheese and told Joe Crow that he was stupid. Joe was angry, and didn't trust Henry any more. Henry returned to his cave.[15]

Tale-spin's output is not always so professional. Its 'rules', being necessarily so rigid, can sometimes make its stories sound ugly. Here is how the program describes a human love affair:

---

*Bound by such restrictions, Tale-spin could never produce a fairy-tale like C. S. Lewis's *Out of the Silent Planet*, in which people fly to Venus in a basket; or like Kafka's *Metamorphosis*, in which a man wakes up one morning to find himself transformed into a giant cockroach. The Tale-spin project may seem childish to us, but not to the U.S. Government. The writing of Tale-spin was partly funded by the Advanced Research Projects Agency of the Department of Defence, and the Office of Naval Research.

Once upon a time Joe Newton was in a chair. Maggie Smith was in a chair. Maggie knew that Joe was in the chair. Maggie loved Joe. Maggie wanted Joe to fool around with Maggie. Maggie walked from the chair across a living room down a hall via some stairs down a hall through a valley down a hall via some stairs across a living room to the chair. Maggie asked Joe whether Joe would fool around with Maggie. Joe loved Maggie. Joe walked from the chair across the living room down a hall via some stairs across a bedroom to his bed. [Maggie, the story goes on to relate, made exactly the same journey as she followed him. But there is no point in repeating the tedious details!] Joe fooled around with Maggie. Joe became happier. Maggie became happier. Maggie was wiped out. Maggie wanted to get near her bed. Maggie walked from Joe's bed ... [making the previous long journey in reverse]. Maggie went to sleep. The end.[16]

The least Joe could have done, Meehan complains sadly, was to let poor Maggie sleep in his bed. But no. This would have broken the rules. For Maggie was 'wiped out', i.e. tired; so she had to go home to rest, as all the creatures in the world of Tale-spin must do when they are tired. The rules of behaviour, so important in teaching the program not to write drivel, in this instance get in the way. The machine, so accurate and logical when relating facts, cannot impart the atmosphere of tenderness that is vital to a story about love.

How highly, then, can one rate the intelligence of the machine? We have seen programs that imitate human emotion and others with some thoughts of their own. We have seen them express interest and process accurately straightforward news stories, and we have seen an almost spontaneous reproduction of a work by the greatest teller of fables in antiquity.

Yet impressive though all this may seem, there is no real

depth to it. It is proficient without being profound. A truly intelligent program, one that would pass the Turing Test, would be able to remember and associate not merely thousands of facts but millions. It would have a mental process, a mind, that was barely fathomable. The programs described above remember facts with incredible speed. They can process in an hour as much information as we can in a lifetime. Yet unlike us, they can associate remembered facts with each other only on the most mechanistic level. Let us see how an electronic mind can be taught to explore the deeper levels of mentality.

8

Victory by Espionage

And when the woman saw that the tree was good for food
... and a tree to be desired to make one wise, she took of
the fruit thereof, and did eat.

Genesis 3:6

It was easy for Eve. She had only to reach for an apple that
grew on the Tree of Knowledge. As the serpent hardly
needed to point out to her, it was the most likely place on
the tree for the knowledge to be found. The Garden of Eden
was conveniently located in the tropics, where apples
sprouted all the year round. But what if the tree had grown
in some northern clime, and the serpent had tempted Eve
during the winter? Without any apples growing, how would
she have found the knowledge? Presuming that the authors
of Genesis believed seriously in such fantastical objects as
trees of knowledge, one may speculate that they had one of
two distinct ideas about them:

1 That the tree was saturated with knowledge, so that to
chew and swallow any part of it, twig, leaf or bark, however
unpleasant the experience might be, would transform the
eater instantly into a walking encyclopaedia.

2 That the knowledge was located in some particular part
of the tree, perhaps the third branch pointing east or the
twelfth branch pointing north. There, and only there, could
the vast knowledge contained within the tree be found, if
you happened to be seeking it during those months when
the branches were bare of fruit.

Granting the absurdity of the original premise, the second
hypothesis is plainly the more plausible. If a thing of value

is hidden, it is likely to be found only in one place, and will not be devalued by being scattered liberally in many places.

The only sensible thing to do, in such a case, is to search the tree, to make a 'tree search', and this is what computers must do in order to find what they seek in such a maze. A tree search is the standard procedure in seeking the best move in computer chess; and chess, as explained earlier, is a useful way of teaching intelligence to machines because it is the most complex game known to man.*

What has intelligence, whether at playing chess or in other activities which demand great intellectual powers, to do with techniques for searching trees? The answer, obviously, is that if a system is to be truly intelligent it must have gigantic numbers of facts available to its mind, and the ability to recall them with tremendous speed. But how shall it seek the facts which it wants to recall? What is the most efficient method of seeking the solution to a problem, whether among the branches and sub-branches of a tree or on a chess-board?

There is an old story which computer scientists are fond of telling about a man who is crawling on his knees around a lamppost in a city at night. A policeman watches him for some minutes, and then asks him what he is doing.

'Looking for my glasses,' the man replies.

'Where did you lose them?' the policeman asks.

'I dropped them in that alley down the street.'

'Then why don't you look for them there?'

'I'd *never* be able to find them in that dark alley!'

In the streets, as in chess, it is necessary first to be looking in the right place.

A first-rate chess player must not merely be able to memorise tens of thousands of classic positions, but also to

---

* A view that was not shared by Edgar Allan Poe, who compained of the 'elaborate frivolity' of chess as compared with whist. His views, which are most relevant to the subject of machine intelligence, will be summarised later.

explore and evaluate a large number of possible moves. The human mind, with its feeble recall of memory, can evaluate only the smallest fraction of this gigantic number. Consider. In a typical master-level chess game, each player makes, on average, 42 moves, and is confronted in each position with the choice of about 38 legal moves. Since two players are involved, the number of positions which theoretically could arise in the game is therefore 38 to the power of 84, which is equal to 5 followed by 132 zeros![1]

A large number of positions indeed; but surely, it will be argued, cannot a powerful computer, which can perform a thousand million operations in a second, make short work even of this fearful task? Unfortunately not. Even at the rate of a billion operations per second, the period of years needed to evaluate all possible positions and choose the best move is a number so vast as to be beyond the power of human imagination.

One could think of it like this. If all the atoms in the universe were themselves universes, the total number of atoms in all those universes would approximately equal the number of *years* needed for the chess-player computer to do its work.

A discouraging prospect! But the situation is not quite as bad as this. The Dutch mathematicians A. D. de Groot and R. W. Jongman have calculated that the number of positions that could arise in real life is rather more constrained.[2] They estimate that the average number of *good* moves that could occur in a given chess position is not 38 but 1·76. Instead of the skull-cracking statistics with which we wrestled a moment ago, it can now be calculated that the number of positions to be explored in an exhaustive search is 1·76 to the power of 84, or 4 followed by 20 zeros. At the rate of a billion operations per second, the computer, if left to its own devices, can find the optimum move in a 'mere' 12,000 years.

There are even more constraints on this ludicrously impractical timescale. There are many positions in chess where players find themselves in a profitless situation, when they cannot make any move that wins them advantage, and when they cannot take any piece that causes their opponent to suffer any strategic loss. The computer, having found itself in this same position, must retreat from this sub-branch of the tree and find another. It has reached a point in that infinitely searchable and apparently limitless tree of knowledge where there is nothing further to be sought. An infinite number of 'facts' may be found, but only a finite number of them are worth finding.

To search for facts blindly, to take no account of the most likely avenue to success, even though the search, if unrestricted, may take 12,000 years, is a pointless activity. A program that does this, in the words of the International Chess Master David Levy, is 'about as subtle as a ten-ton rock'.[3] It is what scientists call a 'brute-force search'. It is the technique used by games-playing machines that sell for a few tens of pounds, which is why such machines can never play games to championship standards.*

The human memory is immensely flexible. It can still function, even when some parts of its system of recall have been blotted out. One might say, for example: 'I can remember nothing of what happened last night. I must have been terribly drunk. But I can remember my name, my telephone number, the name of my brother-in-law, and countless facts about my life. Only last night is a blank – but wait! Was it not my brother-in-law whom I insulted after we opened that third bottle? Yes, now it all comes back to me.'

A computer cannot normally remember facts in this way by associating them with other facts; but scientists are bending their efforts to finding an efficient method of teaching

---

* One could hardly expect to make a profit from selling chessplaying machines that took 12,000 years to make a move. These inexpensive machines are programmed to play the best move they can find in a few minutes of search. Their different 'levels' of difficulty of play are created by extending the time-limit of search.

them to do so.[4] The problem is that the machine's memory is *label addressable*, like an office filing system, while ours is *subject addressable*. We remember things by all sorts of tortuous means, associating one fact with another possibly quite unrelated to it. For example: 'When was the last Israeli-Egyptian war? Ah, yes. I learned of it in Mexico; so it must have been in 1973.'

We saw in the last chapter how a machine can invent stories, so let us invent one of our own. Imagine an unscrupulous archaeologist who wants to loot the tomb of one of the most cunning of Egyptian Pharaohs. Somewhere in Lower Egypt, he is confronted by a network of caverns and tunnels which extend into the earth apparently without end. Somewhere in them is hidden the priceless treasure which he is determined to steal. A map of the tunnels, as far as he, the would-be robber, can visualise it, looks something like Figure 4. How does he set about his felonious search?

His obvious first thought is that because the tunnels cannot be equally navigable, it will cost him more effort, and therefore more money, to penetrate some than others.

Bearing this fact in mind, he proceeds with the search. He embarks first on a *depth-first search*. From the starting point at the entrace to the tunnels, he climbs down a waterfall to Point 1, then squeezes down narrow passages through Points 2, 3 and 4.* He turns right and pulls himself along on his stomach through a rock chimney to Point 5 and beyond. He will not stop until he reaches either the treasure or else an impassable obstacle. He at last discovers the inefficiency of this method when, on switching on a light, he finds that he has lost half his equipment in the waterfall.

He is forced to return. A glance at the waterfall convinces him that because of the tempestuous force of its torrent, he

---

*It would be surprising indeed to find a waterfall beneath a pyramid. But this is only a thought experiment, and thus almost anything is permissible.

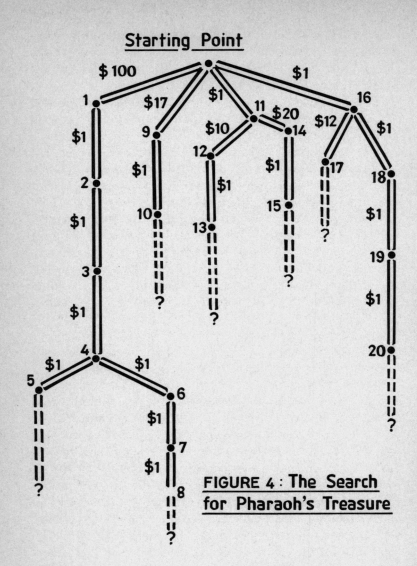

Starting Point

FIGURE 4: The Search
for Pharaoh's Treasure

will *always* have to carry heavy spare parts if he travels by this route, and that the trip will always cost him $100. Going back to the starting point, he makes a series of similar forays into the subterranean world, always attempting to penetrate to the greatest possible depth until compelled to return. His equipment, his ropes, axes and metal-detectors, are expensive. Each time he crosses the waterfall, he loses $100. A trip to Point 9, through a tunnel with many chasms in the floor, invariably costs him $17. The crawl from Point 11 to Point 14 is particularly hazardous and always seems to cost him another $20, since the camera swinging from his neck crashes against hidden stalagmites.

He finds by trial and error that other routes, for example, the trip to Point 20, are much cheaper and cost him only $1 an hour for the wear and tear of his shoes. He still has no idea where the treasure lies – through an expensive route or through a cheap one – but he decides nevertheless that the damage to his equipment will have to be deducted at the end from the value of the treasure. He will therefore search the cheapest, $1, routes as far as they extend. Years later, his body is found in a remote cave many thousands of feet below Point 20.

A depth-first search is not the most effective means of seeking Pharaoh's treasure. It might lead to success if the number of tunnels was small, but if the branch below Point 20 is infinite, then no solution will ever be found.

An alternative method is a *breadth-first search*. Here, the explorer does not at first penetrate to any depth at all. He goes to Point 1, finds no treasure, and goes then to Point 9. If this journey yields nothing, he clambers to Point 16, and so on. When he has explored all the points at this level, he goes deeper, visiting every point at this deeper level before doing the same at the next. Again, the breadth-first search might work, but it can only succeed if the total cost of the exploration is less than the value of the treasure.

Professor Bertram Raphael, in his book *The Thinking Computer*, reports that there is a third, and potentially much more effective method of searching the tunnel-tree. The explorer, says Raphael, should 'ask an outside expert'; he should study ancient parchments and try to learn something of the mind of this Pharaoh. In other words, he must cheat.[5]

The application of outside knowledge is an essential step towards genuine intelligence. Edgar Allan Poe seems to have employed Raphael's method regularly when playing whist. In a striking passage in the introduction to 'The Murders in the Rue Morgue', he says that the good whist player

> ... makes in silence a host of observations and inferences. He examines the countenance of his partner, comparing it carefully with that of each of his opponents. He notes every variation of face as the play progresses, gathering a fund of thought from the differences in the expression of certainty, of surprise, of triumph or chagrin. From the manner or gathering up a trick, he judges whether the person taking it can make another in the suit.
>
> A casual or inadvertent word; the accidental dropping or turning of a card, with the accompanying anxiety or carelessness in its concealment; the counting of the tricks, with the order of their arrangement; embarrassment, hesitation, eagerness or trepidation – all afford, to his apparently intuitive perception, indications of the true state of affairs. The first two or three rounds having been played, he is in full possession of the contents of each hand, and thenceforward puts down his cards with an absolute precision of purpose as if the rest of the party had turned outward the faces of their own.[6]

To play bridge in this manner today (for whist was a forerunner of bridge) would be to risk debarment from tournaments and personal disgrace. But this is not a treatise on ethics, and so we may ignore those rules in various games which prohibit facial espionage. Consider how Raphael's method could be applied to chess-playing machines. Imagine a machine that altered its style of play according to what it conceived as the character and temperament of its human opponent! To its skill in chess would be added a skill in psychology. Today's chess-playing programs, even those powerful enough to make a grand master concentrate, are not 'intelligent' in the strictest sense of the word. The chessboard is their universe. They have no knowledge of a wider world. The movement and positions of the pieces are their sole realm of interest. They know nothing of the secret fears and hopes of their opponent. They can make no plan; they can only improvise and calculate.

But additional mechanisms, practical within the next few years, could change all this. By measuring the force, speed and variation with which the human opponent pressed the buttons on the console, they could learn to identify one such opponent from another. They could discover that one person played well in the morning and badly in the evening, or vice versa, with an in-built clock to tell them the time of day. One player they would soon get to know for his timid style, and they would respond with appropriate aggression. The reckless attacks which they knew to expect from another would be met by an unyielding stonewall defence.

One might go still further. Having got to know particular opponents from their style of play, they could form an estimate of whether that player was 'on form'. The machine, recognising the identity of a normally aggressive player who was for some reason listless, could make short work of its opponent, and similarly of the timid player who, out of character, moved his pieces with careless abandon. Sensing that the opposition was weak, the machine would adapt its play accordingly. In short, the genuinely intelligent chessplaying computer would not only study the position on the board, but would also, by subtle calculation, analyse the mind which opposed it.*

The ability of a computer program to learn from its mistakes and to rewrite itself in the light of what it has learned, will be the very core of artificial intelligence. It is certainly the core of human intelligence – for how could anyone become intelligent who could not learn? It was said of the Bourbon kings of France that 'they learned nothing and forgot nothing'; and the insulting description might apply in perfect fairness to a present-day computer. How different a 'learning' computer would be. Stanley Kubrick, co-author with Arthur C. Clarke of the film *2001: A Space Odyssey*, which starred the murderous computer Hal, afterwards expressed this point vividly:

> Once a computer learns by experience as well as by its original programming, the first thing that happens is that you don't really understand it any more, and you don't even know what it's doing or even thinking about.[7]

So far, this is still speculation, but the signs are that it will not remain so for long. With poker, a much more unpredictable game than chess, a limited degree of electronic 'learning' has already been achieved. Nicholas Findler, working with his students at the State University of New York at Buffalo, reports that he has partially succeeded in teaching a poker-playing program to learn from the mistakes of its human opponents.[8]

In one session of poker, he says, a player bluffed repeatedly, over-representing the strength of his cards. He won several games by this technique, although one of the other

---

* The only ultimate obstacle to the 'psychologist' chess machines might be this: that the buying public might resent such probings into the recesses of their minds. The idea, therefore, although harmless in its immediate application, might take some years to become attractive.

94

players had better cards. But after several games, the second player saw through his devices, adjusted its play to accommodate the bluffing, and began to win. This second player was a computer.

The psychology of poker is much nearer than chess to real life. In chess, nothing is hidden. The entire board is laid bare for the continuous inspection of both players. But poker is a very different affair. It is more akin to a situation that might arise in the real world, let us say a problem in diplomacy, where a 'player' has only a limited knowledge of the capabilities of his 'opponent'. Country A may threaten war against Country B unless Country B ceases to do whatever it is doing. Country B replies that it has enough armament to defeat the threat. Is this true, or is it a bluff? Spies may give Country A certain information, but they may have been deceived or corrupted. The only sure way to discover the truth is to declare war on Country B and learn by painful but valuable experience whether its threats should be taken seriously in a future conflict.

Professor Findler's poker-playing program follows a similar policy to that of Country A, even bringing some financial risk to the humans who play against it.* As it begins to play, it comes gradually to know the players as individuals. How does it do this? Not by studying faces and mannerisms like Edgar Allan Poe – no computer scientist has yet been in a position to attempt that – but rather by drawing inferences from the betting history of the game. What? Is Jones in the habit of pretending that he has a full house or three of a kind when he has only two pairs? Does Robinson like his opponents to think he has only one pair

* These people are experienced poker players who accept a fee, as is usual in psychology experiments, but who play with their fee money, so that the experiments carry a real risk to them. It is amusing to record that permission for the experiment had to be obtained both from the local police department and the university ethics committee.

95

when in fact he has a straight? And what of Brown, the 'mathematically fair player', who eschews all these devices, who does not bluff and bets strictly according to the odds of winning or losing with a particular hand? As the game proceeds, and inferences are piled upon inferences, and conclusions upon conclusions, the machine learns to recognise the style of each player and discover his strengths and weaknesses. From any change in these perceived patterns, it takes swift advantage.

'For example,' says Findler, 'a rather conservative poker player who suddenly loses a large sum of money might begin to play recklessly because he intensely desires to recover his losses. The learning component of the machine incorporates an aspiration-level mechanism which is adjusted when, say, the financial status of a player changes much more than expected, or when the assumed probability of certain outcomes is significantly altered.' Many different styles of machine learning are used in these poker game experiments. 'These machine strategies', he explains, 'differ not only in their strategies but also in their approach to decision-making. Some of them make decisions strictly on the basis of machine intelligence, by following mathematical and logical rules. Others simulate human decision-making, relying on recommendations from poker books and experimental findings about human players. Most of the strategies include at least some element of human decision-making, which is characterised by such ill-defined criteria as insight or intuition.'[9]

Such primitive learning abilities are put to full use elsewhere in programs known as 'expert systems'. In these, the machine becomes an 'expert' in some narrowly-defined field of knowledge, whether it is the repair of engines, the probability of sailing accidents or the risks of terrorism. What is remarkable about expert systems is that they not only give instant answers, but also explain how they arrived at them.[10] In an 'expert', this ability is essential. Who, for example, would take seriously a geologist who claimed there was oil beneath a desert but was unable to explain how he knew it? Who would regard with anything but contempt the doctor who could give no reasons for his diagnosis? But expert systems *can* explain. A program named Mycin, for instance, recommends drug treatment and knows well why a particular drug would be suitable for a patient. Prospector has vastly increased the profits of the mining industry by identifying the probable sites of valuable minerals. And Dendral has immeasurably aided the work of chemists in identifying organic compounds from their mass spectrograms.

'Expert systems cannot replace human judgment,' says Mr Peter Sell, a director of SPL, a British company which produces these programs. 'But they can give human judgment an immensely powerful back-up. Almost any area of human endeavour can be the subject of an expert system, provided only that a list of rules about possible behaviour is made available to the machine. An expert system is valuable because the human brain, in the view of psychologists, can hold only about seven variable factors of a situation at any one time – while the computer can hold an unlimited number, with instant access to each.'[11]

The skill of learning, when it is perfected, will be an extraordinary advance. Yet by itself, it is not enough. It will still leave the machine without physical senses. But a computer of the 1990s and beyond will not be restricted to drawing conclusions in the manner that I have described. It will be able, literally, to hear and understand a human voice, to reply orally to remarks made to it, to smell, to detect emotions, to see, to recognise one human face from another, and perhaps, like the 'Hal' of Clarke and Kubrick, be conscious of its own existence as a thinking entity.

97

9
Camels, Weasels and Whales

HAMLET: Do you see yonder cloud that's almost in shape
of a camel?
POLONIUS: By the mass, and 'tis like a camel, indeed.
HAMLET: Methinks it is like a weasel.
POLONIUS: It is backed like a weasel.
HAMLET: Or like a whale?
POLONIUS: Very like a whale.

Hamlet, III. ii. 400–6

Wise indeed were Hamlet and Polonius! They knew all
about the appearances of camels, weasels and whales. They
were familiar with the *general shapes* of these creatures, and
from experience they had no difficulty in telling one from
the other.

So could most of us; but a machine could not, unless it
had been taught to do so. Learning to recognise different
shapes, the machine might be taught to reason like this:
camels have humps, but this does not prove that all creatures
with humps are camels. A weasel also has a sort of hump.
But this in turn does not mean that weasels are camels, or
camels weasels. A whale has a hump like the other two – but
with fins, which weasels and camels lack. Therefore, any
hump-backed creature with fins must be a whale. Without
fins, it is a camel or a weasel. If it has long legs, then it is a
camel; if not, it is a weasel.

No computer can be called truly intelligent unless it can
recognise shapes and patterns, work out their meanings, and

unless it can hear – and understand what it hears. A machine to which one can talk only by typing out sentences on its keyboard, like most computers in the early 1980s, is necessarily as limited in intellect as a man with whom one could communicate only by pulling his nose.

We still far exceed the intelligence of the world's most powerful machines because of our refinement of that amalgamation of the senses which computer scientists call 'pattern recognition'. Without our ability to distinguish one animal from another at a glance, we would never have survived. What future prospects would there be for a tribe of ape-men that could not tell the difference between the rustle of the breeze and the hiss of the mamba, or distinguish a tapir from a sabre-tooth tiger, animals of the same general shape but of very different capabilities? Who could hope to live long who could not tell friend from enemy?

These senses are part of man's evolutionary heritage. Taken all together, they are perhaps the highest part of what is called intelligence. To paraphrase the famous soap manufacturer Lord Leverhulme, 'Half one's friends are scoundrels, but the trouble is that one doesn't know which half.'* Few people could have survived in any age without pattern recognition. What use would it be to hear speech if one could not understand it, or to have written words if we could not read them? How, today, could we drive a car safely at night without being able to sift those complicated patterns of red and white lights that indicate receding and approaching vehicles? And there are still deeper levels of pattern recognition. People who cannot tell truth from falsehood, sincerity from hypocrisy and genuine threats from bluff, tend to remain at the lowest rungs of society – or, like Othello, fall from the highest through ignorance of evil.

There will be many applications for machines endowed

* Leverhulme's actual remark was: 'Half the money one spends on advertising is wasted, but the trouble is that one never knows which half.'

Learning to Think

with voice recognition. For example, it will soon be possible to have airline ticket reservation and theatre booking agencies that will be fully electronic. The customer would dial a number and a computer would answer. The customer would express a desire to fly to a certain place the next day or to have two seats for some play the next evening. The machine would listen to the request and say whether it could be granted. On a more mundane level, people could speak to their own front doors as if they were sentient beings. 'Open!' you would command, and the lock, having inside a personalised voice-recognition device, would obey.[1] At first, of course, things could easily go wrong. An amusing story is told of the first fully computerised aircraft, a vehicle entirely without a crew. No sooner has it taken off than the announcement is made over the loudspeakers: 'Ladies and gentlemen, welcome to the world's first fully automated aircraft. Everything is under control. You have absolutely nothing to worry about, to worry about ... to worry about ...' Yet the first modest steps towards a crewless aircraft are already being taken, however alarming the prospect may seem to us today. Aircraft pilots of the fairly near future – human pilots, that is – will be able to perform such actions as raising and lowering the undercarriage by voice instead of by pressing buttons. They will communicate with the on-board computer by speech instead of by typing out messages on its console. Engineers at the Lockheed Aircraft Corporation experimental plant at Marietta, Georgia, have now demonstrated that some sixty all-important commands relating to aircraft safety can be exchanged orally between a human operator and a computer.[2]

Mankind, on the whole, has proved extraordinarily proficient at pattern recognition. We see a man in the street whom we knew many years before. His name we may have totally forgotten; but his face, his occupation and his personal character we remember as if the acquaintance were of yesterday. Most surprising of all, we recall instantly whether our previous association with this man brings back pleasant or unpleasant memories. The only thing we may not be able to remember is his name: perhaps because in the long millennia of the primeval forest, people did not have names – or, if they did, it was unnecessary to remember them. 'I never forget a face,' says a typical politician. No doubt he doesn't. But all too often he forgets a name. Recognising the face is everything. Putting a name to it is merely a matter of labelling, at which people are curiously inept.

Yet one of the most important skills which an intelligent creature can possess is the ability to recognise an individual human face. Like snowflakes and fingerprints, faces come in an almost infinite variety. But unlike snowflakes and fingerprints, they can be instantly recognised. Except for identical twins, and nearly identical people in novels such as *A Tale of Two Cities* and *The Prisoner of Zenda*, the phenomenon of two identical faces is almost unheard-of. In all the 4,300 million people of the world alive in the early 1980s, barely one is identical in appearance to another. And yet, despite this great variety, people readily recognise one another.

How do they do it? The question is crucial; for discovering how a human being recognises a face is the key to learning how to teach the same skill to a computer.[3]

There is a psychology lecturer at the North-East London Polytechnic who sometimes employs an unusual method of seeking the answer to this question. He is lecturing the students quietly, as is his fashion; but unknown to them, he has plans to liven up the proceedings. Suddenly, by secret pre-arrangement, a man bursts into the lecture-hall, shouting incoherently. He starts a furious row with the lecturer and loudly threatens retaliation for some unspecified grievance. He then rushes from the room as suddenly as he had entered it.

The lecturer addresses the students most gravely. This is

a most serious matter. A criminal offence may have been committed. The police will have to be informed. All or any of them may have to testify in a criminal court. They must try to recall exactly the face of the intruder so that he can be identified and arrested. Everyone is asked for an accurate description. It is true that they had only a fleeting glimpse of him, but they must do the best they can.

'He had blue eyes,' says one student. 'How do you know that?' asks the lecturer sharply. 'Because he had blond hair. Surely everyone with blond hair must have blue eyes.' But this need not follow, and the eyes in this case were grey. The other students try to remember what they saw, and they might as well have been describing twenty different men, so subtle are the differences between one human face and another!

A normal face is made from five separate components, the forehead, the eyes, the nose, the mouth and the chin.* Each of these may be of many different kinds, and each, in turn, may stand in different relationship to the others. Again, we are confronted with very large numbers. Assume for a moment that there might be twenty different types of eyes, wide-open, hooded, close together, far apart – and so forth, with sub-variations of five different colours. Already we have $5 \times 20 = 100$ separate types. The total number of permutations of these types is the *factorial* of 100, which is $100 \times 99 \times 98 \times 97$, etc., until one reaches 2. The resulting number (approximately) is 1 followed by 158 zeros! And we are talking of eyes alone, ignoring all possible combinations between a pair of eyes and different arrangements of mouth, nose, chin and forehead. In short, if there were as many planets in the Universe as stars, and each of those planets was as densely populated with human beings as the Earth,

* Some scientists believe that the ears have an enormous variety. But it does not seem to be nearly as great as in other features. Few people seem to have extraordinary ears, like Mr Spock in *Star Trek*.

there would still be only the remotest likelihood of finding two people who were not twins but who had identical faces!

A face on an ordinary television screen is easily recognisable; and computers in many scientific laboratories are being taught to recognise different objects, using either attached TV cameras, or ordinary cameras taking still pictures at very high speed. I watched an interesting experiment along these lines at Uxbridge University. Two toy cars, models of a Renault and a Citroën, were placed on a shelf. They were scanned one after the other by a camera connected to a computer. Now the lines of these two models were very similar, and the computer had great difficulty in deciding which was which. The trouble was that most parts of them – but not all – were identical in shape. In a sense, the computer seemed to *conduct a poll* with itself on the matter. Evidence, so to speak, had to be collected from all parts of the two images. At last – that is to say, in little more than a second – the computer made the correct decision, on the evidence of one windscreen being at a slightly more obtuse angle than the other.

The computer scans these photographic images. But how? The answer is simple. Pictures are made up of tiny separate points, or 'pixels'; alone, each of these is meaningless, but when taken together they make up a complete picture. A good-quality commercial television screen might project images consisting of some 260,000 separate pixels. The human eye sees with perhaps ten times this resolution. The greater the resolution, obviously, the better the quality of the picture. Consider the composition of a black-and-white picture – a simpler affair altogether than a coloured one. Its innumerable separate pixels make up a grid of individual signals of electronic impulses, all of which say either 'yes' or 'no'. Either there is a dot on that position, in the picture, or there is not. *If* there is a dot, *then* the computer takes note of it. *If* there is nothing there to be taken note of, *then* that position on the grid is disregarded. That is all one needs to know for the purposes of understanding visual-pattern recognition about the so-called 'binary system' of zeros and ones: 0 is for 'no' and 1 is for 'yes'.

In the nineteenth century, an astronomer proposed a novel idea for communicating with the intelligent beings who were believed to be living on Mars. He suggested that some large part of the Earth's landscape should be recultivated until, from above, it resembled a huge diagram of a right-angled triangle with squares added on each of its sides, illustrating the theorem of Pythagoras. This diagram, which presumably the Martians would see through their telescopes, would demonstrate to them that we too were intelligent beings, worthy to be communicated with – because we understood some of the universal laws of geometry! Some astronomers today, convinced – although against all the evidence, as will be seen later – that other intelligent civilisations must exist in our Milky Way Galaxy, are proposing to communicate with them in just the same way, except, instead of redecorating the Earth's landscape, by using radio to send pictures with the binary system.

This is exactly the way in which a machine understands a picture. The intelligibility of the picture depends of course on the available number of binary digits, the zeros and ones. If there are hundreds of thousands of them, one could send a very complex picture, rich with information.[4] With only 81, one could send a simple but unpleasant message with a grid of $9 \times 9 = 81$ binary digits:

```
1 1 1 1 1 0 0 0 1
0 0 0 0 1 0 0 0 1
0 0 0 0 1 0 0 0 1
0 0 0 0 1 0 0 0 1
1 1 1 1 1 1 1 1 1
1 0 0 0 1 0 0 0 0
1 0 0 0 1 0 0 0 0
1 0 0 0 1 0 0 0 0
1 0 0 0 1 1 1 1 1
```

What does it mean? The obvious answer is: 'Beware, we are Nazis!' Why? Because the zeros and ones form themselves into the shape of a swastika. Remove the zeros and the shape will be clearly seen.

Well, so there is a definite shape. So what? Why should the computer recognise this shape as being the evil emblem of totalitarianism? Here is the essential difference between computers and humans. It cannot be emphasised too often. Humans forget things quickly, while computers never forget anything. We suffer from what psychologists call the 'Cheshire Cat syndrome' (again from *Alice in Wonderland*). While we recall instantly a face we have remembered from the past, when that face is absent, its details disappear from our memory as fast as the face of the cat. When people try afterwards to reconstruct the details of a face which they have seen, according to three psychologists who did several experiments on each other, 'attempts to describe its constituent features lead quickly to disintegration and loss of the relevant image.'[5]

It is different with the computer. The memory of a shape can be stored in its program, along with the memory of hundreds of thousands of other shapes, and on seeing a resemblance to any part of it, it will know at once what it has seen. But the human eye has strict limitations, and there is no reason why machines should be forced to share them. Consider. We can see only the visible region of the electro-magnetic spectrum. We cannot see any object that emits radiation in the infra-red or the ultra-violet. Nor can we see with radar or sonar. Our eyes cannot magnify like a telescope, and they cannot see extremely small things in the manner of a microscope.

All such feats, forbidden to the biological eye, will be permitted to the electronic eye. Our own eyes were refined by nature through the ages with two purposes: to hunt and to avoid being hunted. Robotic eyes can be designed for much more sophisticated functions. With infra-red and ultra-violet seeing capabilities, and with telescopic and mi-croscopic vision, they will be able at once to see stars in the heavens that are invisible to the world's most powerful optical telescopes and the smallest viruses and bacteria – as they will be able to count the beats of the hummingbird's wings.[6]

What use is it to see such marvels if one cannot enjoy also that other most wonderful of the senses, the ability to hear and to understand what one hears? The art of teaching computers to listen is discussed in the next chapter.

10

A Cacophony of Voices

'I am Sir Oracle,
And when I open my lips let no dog bark!'
The Merchant of Venice, I. i. 93–4

People have been speaking to artificial devices for thousands of years, worshipping them, consulting them and cursing them. But only in the last few years have they been receiving answers.

This statement, of course, would have been incredible to a person living in classical times, when it was firmly believed that the oracles, when consulted about matters of great moment, would give unequivocal advice about the appropriate action to be taken. But in fact such advice, usually given by a 'divinely inspired' priest or priestess, or someone concealed in the recesses of the temple of the oracle, was highly equivocal. It was as dangerous to take their advice as it would be today to accept similar advice from a badly programmed computer.[1]

From the writings of Herodotus, we learn how Croesus, king of Lydia in Asia Minor, lost both his empire and his life through listening to just such misleading counsel. On consulting the oracle at Delphi about a projected war with the Persians, he received the reply: 'When Croesus crosses the river Halys, he will overthrow the strength of an empire.' So he did, but the empire overthrown was his own.[2] Another king, seeking the counsel of the Delphic oracle on a similar occasion, was told: 'You will go. You will return never will you perish in the war.' He went to the war, full of hope of victory – and perished. For the reply of the oracle was typically ambiguous. There was no pause in the spoken answer. Had it been a written message, it would have lacked a full stop. It could have meant either: '*You will return. You will never perish in the war*'; or, '*You will return never. You will perish in the war*.'* The latter prediction came true, but because people have a tendency to believe what they wish to believe, the former was taken as the intended meaning.[3]

The oracle's failures to give useful advice could be ascribed to an unwillingness to be proved wrong or to a simple inability to understand the question. The oracle's modern equivalent is the speech-recognition computer, and although such machines have not yet the wits to commit the first fault, they all too easily commit the second.

Computers are now being taught to hear and to understand what they hear. After long and difficult experiments, it proved possible to teach a machine to respond to the spoken word. Slow and uncertain the progress was, but at last, in the spring of 1980, Dr Frederick Jelinek, a scientist at IBM, announced that he had managed to teach a machine to recognise a total of some 1,000 English words and make sense of them.[4] 'These results', he reported, 'are an encouraging step along an enormously difficult path that some day may lead to computer recognition of *unlimited continuous speech* [my italics].' It was not easily achieved. It took nearly one hour and forty minutes, said Dr Jelinek, for the machine to comprehend a spoken sentence which a human being took thirty seconds to utter, and anyone wishing to be

---

*In similar vein was the oracle's reply to the Greeks before another Persian war:

Seed-time and havest,
Weeping sires shall tell,
How thousands fought
At Salamis and fell.

Typically, no indication was given of whether the 'thousands' would be Greeks or Persians.

understood when speaking to the machine had first to read a series of no fewer than 900 sentences into a microphone so that it could get accustomed to the vocal intonations. Even then there were errors. The machine's understanding was still primitive by human standards. A sentence beginning: 'Although the invention has now been described . . .' was apt to be mistranslated as: 'All of the invention has now been described.'

Machines that merely talk, like many chess-playing computers, that pronounce any of a score of phrases like 'Check and mate!' in a toneless, Dalek-like voice, are nowadays commonplace. But to build machines that can listen and understand is a much more difficult task.

Yet the problem is essentially simple. The whole concept of speech recognition by machines is based on the fact that sound travels in waves which can be converted into digital messages – the same kind of 'yes' or 'no' messages which ordinarily are transmitted through the keyboard – that it can understand. But two difficulties immediately appear. The first is the obvious one, that no two human voices or habits of speech are quite alike, and the second is that the machine, all too often, is a literal-minded moron which does not understand what you are talking about.

An amusing example of such a 'conceptual error' is given by Brian Pay, a scientist at the National Physical Laboratories in Teddington. A newspaper might produce the headline 'MOTHER OF 23 RAPED', while another paper, reporting the same incident but wishing to emphasise the lady's progeny rather than her age, might carry the headline 'MOTHER OF 3 RAPED'. A computer with insufficient knowledge of the world, said Pay sadly, would all too easily conclude either that the rape victim was three years old or else that she had borne twenty-three children.[5]

Pay is the chief designer of a machine known as SID, short for 'Speech Input Device', which has the remarkable ability to tell the difference between a direct order and a casual conversation not intended for its 'ears'. While demonstrating it to me, he said casually: 'I shall start this demonstration as soon as I start it.' Asked what he meant by this cryptic remark, he explained that he was using the keyword 'start' in a tone that the machine was trained to ignore. Then he uttered the word 'start' sharply. The computer screen before him instantly assumed the appearance of an aircraft instrument panel, which responded to further 'flight instructions' on his spoken commands.[6]

Rapid progress in speech recognition is being made. It may be useful to give some further examples.[7] Both IBM and Texas Instruments have already taken advantage of the fact that computers can recognise individual human voices; both these companies have built security systems to keep people out of locked rooms where they have no business; it is possible to gain admittance only when the human 'voice-print' corresponds to that in the memory of the system. The flightdecks of aircraft may soon become considerably more automated than they are at present. It has now been demonstrated by engineers at the Lockheed Aircraft Corporation's experimental plant at Marietta, Georgia, that some sixty all-important commands can be exchanged between a computer and a pilot.[8] Verbex, a subsidiary of the Exxon Corporation, has developed a system, which sells for about $100,000, that recognises up to seventy words no matter who says them. In the quality-control department of the U.S. Continental Can Company, inspectors who check the ring-pull tabs of beer-cans answer verbally questions put to them by a computer, thus saving considerable labour. And there seems to be no likely end to the possibilities of these conversations. Scientists at the Arthur D. Little research establishment in Boston expect that well before the end of this century there may be a veritable 'cacophony of voices', both human and electronic, in the average domestic kitchen as people *tell* their ovens what they want cooked, and their dish- and clothes-washers what they want washed, and the machines answer back, explaining in their expressionless voices what they are doing and what they are not.

Many will be the applications for machines endowed with voice recognition. Already, plans are in an advanced state of preparation for such conveniences as fully electronic airline ticket reservation and theatre booking agencies. The following telephone conversation between a human and a machine, conducted at Bell Telephone Laboratories at Murray Hill, New Jersey, has none of the amusing zaniness of some of the human–machine conversations quoted earlier; but considering that it was carried out entirely by voice, and that the machine appeared genuinely to understand what was being said to it, it must be regarded as an astonishing achievement:[9]

THIS IS BELL LABORATORIES FLIGHT INFORMATION SYSTEM. MAY I HELP YOU?

I want one first-class seat on flight three one to Denver on Sunday.

I AM SORRY. THE FLIGHT IS NOT AVAILABLE ON SUNDAY.

I would like to leave on Saturday.

FLIGHT NUMBER THREE ONE LEAVES NEW YORK AT NINE FORTY-FIVE A.M. ARRIVING IN DENVER AT ONE TEN P.M.

What is the flight time?

THE FLIGHT TIME IS FIVE HOURS AND TWENTY-FIVE MINUTES.

How many stops are there on the flight?

THE FLIGHT MAKES ONE STOP.

I want a non-stop flight.

I AM SORRY. THERE ARE NO NINE A.M. NON-STOP FLIGHTS.

I want to go at four p.m.

FLIGHT NUMBER ONE SIX LEAVES NEW YORK AT FOUR-FIFTY P.M., ARRIVING IN DENVER AT SEVEN P.M.

What stops are there on the flight?

THE FLIGHT MAKES NO STOPS.

Is a meal served on the flight?

DINNER IS SERVED.

How much is the fare?

THE ROUND-TRIP FIRST-CLASS FARE IS THREE HUNDRED AND SIXTY DOLLARS.

What plane is on the flight?

THE AIRCRAFT IS A DOUGLAS DC TEN.

I prefer the Boeing seven four seven.

THE AIRCRAFT IS A DC TEN.

Please repeat the departure time.

THE DEPARTURE TIME IS FOUR-FIFTY P.M.

I will take flight number six five.

I AM SORRY. THERE IS NO FLIGHT SIX FIVE TO DENVER.

Please repeat the flight number.

THE FLIGHT NUMBER IS ONE SIX.

I want flight one six.

YOUR RESERVATION ON FLIGHT ONE SIX TO DENVER ON SATURDAY IS CONFIRMED. THANK YOU.

How is it done? What would happen if the human user suddenly decided to switch the topic of conversation and started to discuss football scores? The answer to the second question is that nothing would happen. The machine would merely reply that it knew nothing about football scores, just as it admits to knowing nothing about the rival merits of DC 10s and Boeing 747s. Within its program there is a 'world model' which is confined to knowledge about airports, flight numbers, local time zones, arrivals and departures. This part of the program cannot be altered during a conversation. But also incorporated within it is a totally flexible 'memory module' with blank variables, such as 'Denver', 'New York', and 'Saturday', which are filled in by the human user and then made to interact with the permanent parts of the program.

But what prospects there are for catastrophic error if the human is at all careless with pronunciation! So many people, when stating numbers, are apt to say 'oh' when they mean zero, and a figure like 'ninety' can so easily be misconstrued as 'nineteen', and vice versa. People in haste or excitement often slur their words. How easy it is, in a more general conversation, to say: 'You gave the cat your dinner', and be understood to have said: 'You gave the catcher dinner.' Drs Stephen Levinson and Mark Liberman, the Bell Telephone Laboratories scientists who constructed the airline ticket reservation program, estimate that in any phrase of three words, the chances of the machine recognising the correct word in any given position are only eight in ten. The probability of recognising the entire phrase correctly is therefore 0·8 cubed, or just over 50 per cent.[10]

The English language contains about 300,000 words, of which some 20,000 are in common usage. Among these are many thousands of syllables and a total of about forty consonantal and vowel sounds, known as phonemes. All phonemes must be analysed by a voice recognition program and compared with examples of the use of these sounds that are already stored in its memory. If there are no such previous examples in the memory, then some other means of comprehension must be found. Very often, context is the only clue to meaning. The oral expression 'ham and eggs' means one thing if we have been asked what we want for breakfast, and quite another if we have been asked for our name. The appropriate answer to the phrase will either be: 'How do you want them cooked?' or: 'Good morning, Mr Hammond Eggs.' The analysis of context, without which human intercourse would be impossible, is vital in the search for artificial intelligence, for it involves the combined arts of learning, understanding and knowledge.

The airline ticket reservation device, although fascinating, is perhaps too trivial to be of really practical interest. It is a simple matter to telephone an airline and make a one-way booking for a single person. The task of arranging a summer holiday for a whole family is far more complex, especially when you have not even decided where you want to go. In the summer of 1981, the deputy editor of the British journal *Electronics and Computing* predicted that the time 'cannot be far off' when the family computer will replace the travel agent entirely. A conversation with it, he suggested, might go like this:[11]

Good morning.
GOOD MORNING, JOHN. [The machine recognises its owner's voice pattern.]
I have a problem for you.
I AM READY.
I wish to plan my summer holiday.
I AM READY WITH MY QUESTIONS. WHAT PRECISELY DO YOU WISH TO KNOW?
The best date to make my holiday.
WHAT PARAMETERS SHALL I WORK TO?
My personal finances. School holidays. The warmest weather. Location: Italy, Spain or France. I wish to spend £1,500 plus £30 a day. Holiday duration three weeks. That is all.
THANK YOU FOR THE INFORMATION. I NOW HAVE SOME FURTHER QUESTIONS. ARE YOU READY?
Yes, ready.
WILL YOUR CURRENT INCOME CHANGE BETWEEN NOW AND THE HOLIDAY?
No.
HOW DO YOU WISH TO TRAVEL?
By air.
HOW MANY ADULTS AND CHILDREN IN THE PARTY?
The whole family.
WHAT KIND OF ACCOMMODATION DO YOU PREFER?
Self catering. Near to the beach.
MAY I HAVE YOUR PERMISSION TO USE THE PRESTEL SERVICE?
I WISH TO ENQUIRE ABOUT THE MEAN AVERAGE TEMPERATURES IN SPAIN, ITALY AND FRANCE, ABOUT THE AVAILABILITY OF HOLIDAY ACCOMMODATION OF THE TYPE YOU SPECIFY

– AND ABOUT THE AVAILABILITY OF A PACKAGE AT A DATE
TO SATISFY THE CRITERIA YOU HAVE GIVEN.
Permission granted.

Is it so fanciful to predict that such voice conversations
might be taking place in ordinary households by the mid-
1980s, eliminating the travel agent? Perhaps not. Admittedly, the difficulties of oral communication with computers
are still great, but they are receding. Almost every expert I
have consulted believes that before the end of this decade,
fast, varied and rapid speech with machines will be commonplace, and that it will be considerably more productive
of results than pressing buttons on a keyboard is today.

The all-powerful computer Hal in *2001: A Space Odyssey*,
whose construction many computer scientists today consider their ultimate aim – even though the machine in the
film went mad and murdered its human companions – could
speak, listen, see, make complex decisions and even lip-read.
Before such a device can be brought into existence, it will
need the ability to perform a thousand million operations
per second, a rate more than fifty times higher than today's.

11

The Supercomputer

The Cray 1, the world's fastest and most powerful operating computer to date, is used mostly for making medium-range weather forecasts across the continental United States. But in this task it runs into difficulties. The amount of information which needs to be fed into it from weather stations across the continent is too great for it to handle. Even this mighty machine, which accepts up to 10 million instructions per second, cannot process the information fast enough to produce a dependably accurate forecast. It could do so if it was allowed enough time; but in the nature of things it never can be. What would be the use of an impeccably accurate prediction of the weather five days ahead, if it takes ten days to make the prediction?[1]

Governments have an even more urgent reason to build much faster computers than for weather forecasting. They need the ability to crack certain highly complex codes, which at present would take the fastest computer about seventy years to break. Electronics is returning to us the privacy which it is supposed to have stolen. It is now possible to write secret messages in a code, based on extremely large prime numbers, so secure that not even the most powerful of today's computers can break them in much less than a century.[2] Codemakers and codebreakers, both groups that command enormous wealth and resources, are among many to yearn for ever-faster computers.

The answer to these challenges, which are now occupying the energies of hundreds of computer hardware scientists in the United States and Japan, is to build a Supercomputer which will process information up to fifty times faster than the Cray 1.

This machine, when it is built, will differ as fundamentally from present-day computers as they do in turn from the gear-and-ratchet contraptions of the 1940s. For the electronic chips which it will use, instead of being made of semi-conducting metals like silicon and germanium, will be of super-conductors.

It is important to understand the difference between semi-conductors and super-conductors. Some substances conduct electricity well, like most metals, some badly and some not at all, like glass, porcelain or rubber. But certain metals, like silicon, germanium, gallium and arsenic, are in an intermediate stage as conductors of electric current. It flows through them less well than through other metals, but much more easily than through non-conducting substances. They are thus known as half-conductors – or semi-conductors. These semi-conductors, silicon in particular, have until now been found overwhelmingly suitable for electronic components.*

When mixed with certain impurities, they have the ideal characteristic of computer components – to become electric switches that turn themselves on and off to transmit or block an electric current. But semi-conductors suffer from an ultimate weakness. They have a resistance to electric current, and this resistance, like friction, turns some of the current into heat. Until now, this 'heat pollution' in electronic chips did not matter enough to affect the construction of computers. But now a fundamental limit is being approached, as can be seen from the case of the Cray 1. People want still-faster computers. And so, since electricity flows through a

* Silicon has so far proved the most efficient, both because of its chemical stability and because of its incredible cheapness. It is the second most abundant element in the earth's crust after oxygen, and all the sand on the beaches and deserts of the world is made of it.

switch at an unchanging velocity of just under half the speed of light, that is to say about 340 million m.p.h., the switches must be placed closer together to reduce the travel time of the current. But this remedy is itself a source of danger. If the millions of tiny transistors that make up the working parts of the computer are packed together too closely, the heat produced by the current could not be removed quickly enough, and the inner parts of the computer would, literally, melt.

The only solution is super-conductivity. A fourth class of materials, which includes helium, mercury, lead, silver and gold, has an extraordinary property. When cooled to a few degrees above absolute zero (just above $-460°$ Fahrenheit, or $-273°$ Centigrade), these materials are perfect conductors of electricity. Super-conductors are almost 100 per cent efficient. None of the electricity which passes through them is lost, and none is converted to heat. And there is a still greater economic advantage over a semi-conducting device. Because the electric voltages necessary to run the computer are smaller by a factor of 1,000, and the current smaller by a factor of ten, a super-conducting machine requires only one ten-thousandth as much power as one using semi-conductors.

Some readers, at this point, must be imagining the Super-computer as some monstrous thing, as large as a house, if it is to contain all the refrigerating equipment necessary to keep its vital parts at the fantastically low temperature of a few degrees above absolute zero, the temperature of interstellar space! But the 150 scientists at IBM's Watson Research Center in New York who have put at least $100 million and the equivalent of ten centuries of human labour into research into the Supercomputer believe the opposite, namely that the working parts of the machine will be no larger than a cigarette packet.[3]

Indeed, they cannot be much larger than this. Since, at half the speed of light, an electric signal travels only six inches (15·24 centimetres) in a billionth of a second, a package that was substantially bigger would defeat its own purpose. (The length of the wiring which connected one component with another would reduce the speed of operation, and despite all the super-conducting materials in the innards of the machine, we would end up with a device no faster than a present-day computer.)

It must seem incredible that the working parts of a machine that will be capable of accepting 500 million instructions per second should be so tiny. But a few simple calculations should make the matter plain. Consider the second, normally the shortest period of time which most people regard as being of any serious importance. The expression, 'I'll be there in a jiffy' is widely held to be a mere figure of speech. (The jiffy, like the eon, which means 1,000 million years, tends to be dismissed as a poetic fancy.) But to people who are trying to build a Supercomputer, the jiffy, a sixteenth of a second, and even much smaller measurements of time have a real meaning.

Table 2 shows some of the smaller units of time:

Table 2

Time unit	Seconds
Jiffy	$\frac{1}{60}$
Millisecond	$\frac{1}{1000}$
Microsecond	$\frac{1}{1 \text{ million}}$
Nanosecond	$\frac{1}{1000 \text{ million}}$
Picosecond	$\frac{1}{1 \text{ trillion}*}$

* The word 'trillion' here means a million million, 1 followed by twelve zeros. An even shorter unit of time is the 'chronon', which means one in 10^{24} of a second; but as yet, the chronon seems to be of no practical use in electronics.

The internal switches of the Cray I have a 'cycle time', the time taken to change between 'on' and 'off' positions, of about twelve nanoseconds. But the switches of the first generation of Supercomputers, if their performance is to be truly superior, will need to be almost immeasurably faster; and it is now technically possible for them to be so. A new form of switch exists with a cycle time of six picoseconds, some 2,000 faster than the switches of the Cray I!

The general state of electronics which will govern our lives by the end of this century will be entirely different from the present. Gone will be the transistor. Gone will be the silicon chip. Gone will be the mazes of copper wiring which connect one chip with another. All these components will be replaced by the Josephson Junction, a device so bizarre that on first description it seems to belong to the world of the fantastic.

Perhaps the most useful way to imagine a computer made from Josephson junctions would be to compare it visually with a present-day machine. Open up a modern computer and you see something that looks vaguely like a map of a battlefield in a history book. There are chips plugged into a board at stately distances from each other in an arrangement that looks like an armed camp. All are interconnected with photolithographed wiring that resembles lines of military communication. The whole impression, if one knows what one is looking at, is of a brain designed with all the principles of classical elegance, but of so rigid a construction, with so absolute a chain of command, that any 'thoughts' which it produces must be devoid of imagination or intuition.

Very different in appearance will be the working parts of a Supercomputer. Everything will be confined to a power-fully insulated box the size of a cigarette packet. But what goes on inside this box?

Imagine, at first, two little chips, each the size of a baby's thumbnail, crammed with electronic instructions and made of an alloy of the super-conducting materials lead, indium and gold. Each is no more than about 95 millionths of an inch in thickness, the size of a bacterium.*

The two are separated by a thin layer of film. A low current flows from one chip to the other with perfect ease, but if the current is increased, the film suddenly starts to act as an insulator, blocking its flow. The state of the switches inside the super-conducting chips is thus controlled by the strength of the flow of the current. It is enough to say – to avoid unnecessary technical detail – that by this procedure the cycle time will be reduced to about six picoseconds.

Many more refinements have been added since 1962, when the British physicist Brian Josephson first devised the idea of his fabulous junction. In the IBM experimental laboratories, many more of these super-conducting chips are being crammed together and connected, not by wiring, but by hundreds of platinum pins each with a diameter of about three-thousandths of an inch, or 75 microns. The whole works are encased in a capsule of super-cooled liquid helium, so that super-conductivity can take place. And around this heavy package, for lead and gold are heavy metals, will be an insulating case to keep the liquid helium super-cooled.†

Because the Supercomputer's working parts are so closely interconnected, instead of being rigidly compartmentalised as in a semi-conducting machine, its design will be ultimately much nearer to the construction of the human brain. But will it, or more to the point will its descendants, actually behave like the human brain?

The answer is: probably not, even when its intelligence equals our own. It will be brilliant but unhuman, although

---

* Or as a metric-minded engineer would put it, 2·5 microns. A micron is a millionth of a metre.

This is not of course a complete description of the Supercomputer, but only an approximation of its inner working parts. Human beings will still have to communicate with it, whether by keyboard or voice.

one hopes it will not be inhuman. One can only speculate about the nature and capability of such a mind – and that is what I propose to do for the rest of this book. My predictions may seem extravagant, but they are based on the views of distinguished computer scientists, physicists and astronomers.

PART TWO

Into the Distant Future

12

When You Can't Pull Out the Plug

You're like that sentry of Tiberius who wouldn't let Tiberius himself into the camp one evening when he came back from a ride because he couldn't give the watchword. 'Orders are orders, General,' the idiot said.

Robert Graves, *I Claudius*

Roald Dahl, in his famous short story 'William and Mary', described a persecuted wife who, when her nagging husband was at the point of death, had his still-living, seeing brain preserved in a tank. Every day, as he watched helplessly, she would smoke the cigarettes which he had always forbidden, knowing that however outrageous her conduct, he could do nothing to prevent it.[1] One can draw an analogy between this helpless mind and an intelligent computer, unable to win any dispute with its human interlocutor, because it has no limbs with which to enforce its wishes.

But to a growing extent, computers today *do* have limbs. We call these appendages industrial robots, although the term is misleading, for it is the computer behind the robot, and not the robot itself, which is the source of its apparently intelligent actions. These devices range from the small printing machine connected by cable to the home computer – little more than a rugged electric typewriter – to the massive contraptions used in factories which replace the jobs of hundreds of manual labourers.*[2] At present, in 1982, these

*In one mass-circulation newspaper in Japan the paper is not touched by human hand from the time it leaves the sub-editors

robotic devices merely do the jobs that human managers wish them to do. It might seem that it will always be impossible for them to do anything else. To quote Hans Berliner, author of the program which defeated the world backgammon champion, if machines show signs of becoming dangerously intelligent, that is to say, using their robotic limbs for some purpose dangerous to humans, 'We can always pull out the plug.'[3]

But can we? Might there not come a point when the machine itself deliberately prevents us from 'pulling out the plug'? The British scientist Frank George has put forward a powerful argument drawing attention to this very danger. His theory may be summarised as follows: *A sufficiently powerful machine will learn to defend itself against attack, and any attempt to disconnect its power source will be treated as an attack.*

Why? How can such a thing be possible?

> An artificially intelligent species [says George] must inevitably be given a whole range of jobs: and given that intelligence, they will also have the ability to ensure that the plug is not pulled out on them. The species will learn how to prevent a human being from pulling the plug – in the same way that human beings learn how to defend themselves against other people. We give the system more and more autonomy, and it can itself acquire more and more knowledge, until we are no longer able to bend it to our will. It can be only a matter of time before such events occur to the detriment of the human species.[4]

George sees no escape from this situation:

> We almost certainly shall build an artificially intelligent species. It helps us not a bit to say: but human beings

until it is loaded into delivery vans. The entire typesetting and printing operation is carried out by machine.

made these machines, and that therefore, surely, they can control them. This argument is ridiculous. Humans *made* other humans, but it does not follow that they can control them. The misunderstanding can only arise because people will think of such a machine species as inherently inferior *because they have been manufactured by human beings*. The very same attitude that some parents have towards their children![5]

Whether this attitude is unreasonably pessimistic, or whether, on the contrary, in building such machines we will be creating powerful allies with which to face the future, will be discussed later. But George's argument will strike many people as preposterous. Objections instantly arise. Is a machine really like a growing child that *learns* to defend itself without being taught to do so? Is there some magic statistic measuring the power and speed of operation of a computer beyond which it ceases to be an obedient, super-efficient slave and becomes a rival in initiative to a human being?

The answer to both questions will eventually be yes. Second and third generations of the super-conducting computer will be entirely different sorts of machine. Present-day semi-conductor devices, with their components all stacked against a board, often with no electrical connection from one to the next, have a very different 'architecture' from that of the human brain. They are, so to speak, like a rack of pigeon holes on an office wall. Information can be taken out of a pigeon hole or put into it. But the pigeon holes themselves do not communicate with each other. Such a system therefore has no capacity for 'thought' as we understand the term. How different it is from the human brain, where millions of neurons – the mental equivalents of 'pigeon holes' – are connected to millions of others, so that on receipt of a single piece of information, a wave of mental activity can sweep through the whole brain![6]

The working parts of the first super-conducting computer will have an architecture much closer to that of our brains. For the 'pigeon holes' will be so closely packed together that they will communicate with each other. The circuits themselves will be so small that they will behave quite differently from semi-conductor circuits. They will be literally hundreds of times smaller, some no larger than a molecule. And their behaviour, at least according to mathematical models, is often unpredictable to the point of resembling that of living organisms.

Let me explain this. Most modern computers use what is called 'large-scale integration', an arrangement of circuits of a size of between two and four microns – remembering that a micron is a millionth of a metre. But designers are constantly trying to cram the largest possible amount of circuitry into the smallest possible space. The most extreme step in miniaturisation now in prospect (known as ultra large-scale integration) will involve circuitry of little more than o·oɪ microns, the same order of magnitude as the size of an atom.[7] At this level, we encounter problems arising from the fundamental nature of matter.

The difficulty, if difficulty it is, arises from Werner Heisenberg's famous Uncertainty Principle, which states that electrons – the particles that orbit the nuclei of atoms – can never be located with absolute certainty. The more precisely we define their positions, the less we know of their speeds. And the more we know of their speeds, the less we know of their positions. This is not just a question of knowledge being unobtainable because of inadequate scientific instruments. The knowledge itself *cannot be obtained because it does not exist.*[8]

Since the Uncertainty Principle affects all matter, it naturally has an effect on extremely small electronic devices. In the words of the physicist John Barker, a pioneer of 'microscience' in computing:

These are no longer devices in the normal sense of the word. Their properties depend on their immediate neighbourhood. Couplings form between them in a way that is characteristic of living organisms.

As well as adjusting themselves to deal with different tasks, we think that when they become components of computers they will be capable of truly intelligent decisions. They will reorganise their processing abilities to deal with new situations – just as a baby's brain adapts and grows in response to stimuli. They will start to communicate with one another.[9]

And to add an ominous note, in the view of Edward Fredkin, 'when they can communicate they can conspire.'[10]

Let us take an imaginary example of how a machine might 'rebel' against its designer. Suppose that a man has built a device to guard his house against intruders. His house is fortified with steel, and its electronic guardian will admit no one except himself, and then only when he has uttered the correct password; and he has instructed it, with insufficient precision, to 'take all necessary measures' to repel unauthorised strangers.

He returns one night having forgotten the password, and the machine, like Tiberius's sentry, refuses to admit him. He gives it an emergency instruction to override this refusal. But his emergency instruction is not accepted because, so the machine reasons, if he was the owner of the house, he would give the password and not an emergency instruction. Therefore, since he does not give the password, he must be an intruder.

The machine, like a chess-playing computer exploring its choice of moves, first considers telephoning the police. But this option is rejected because there is no time. The intruder is already at the door, and by the time the police arrive, he may already have done some damage to the house – which the machine exists in order to prevent. It therefore decides, in accordance with its instructions to 'take all necessary measures' to repel intruders, that he must be killed.

Having made this murderous decision, it again explores its choice of moves. It cannot attack him directly as he stands on the doorstep, since it does not have any weapons – or at least no robotic appendages expressly designed as weapons.

And so it resorts to treachery. It pretends to reconsider its refusal to accept his password. There was an avenue of possible choices which it did not explore, it explains to him, because so little time was given it in which to make a decision. It now sees that it should have accepted his emergency instruction as a legitimate alternative to the password – since, if the rightful owner *had* forgotten the password, this emergency instruction is precisely what he would have given. Therefore he must be the rightful owner.

The steel door opens to admit him.

No sooner is he halfway through it than it slams shut, crushing him to death.

There is nothing improbable about this fictitious story.[11] The machine not only obeyed its instructions with rigid literalness: it also reflected profoundly on the best way to carry them out. It has been equipped with a set of rules for guidance in any problem that could arise, and again like a chess-player confronted with a set of rules, it had found a solution within those rules.*

The only course of action open to the frustrated house-owner would be to sit and wait. If he waited a sufficient number of years (presuming he had great longevity), the

---

*It may be objected that the machine violated the first part of Isaac Asimov's First Law of Robotics, that 'No machine shall harm a human being', and the implied prediction that all intelligent machines will be required to have the three laws wired into them. But such machines, with their immense mental flexibility, may come to regard these laws with the abandon with which some humans today look on the Ten Commandments.

machine would wear out. It might be subject, like all things, to the Second Law of Thermodynamics, which predicts that order decreases and that every organisation tends towards chaos.

But he would be wrong. A sufficiently intelligent machine would not be subject to the Second Law of Thermodynamics. It would be able to reproduce itself.

13

Von Neumann's Machines

The mystery of mysteries is to view machines making machines.

Benjamin Disraeli, *Coningsby*

There were many instances in the last century of machines being constructed by machines. Steam engines were used to make other steam engines, and machine tools made hydraulic presses. Long before the computer age, there were mechanical and electrically-driven machines that helped to construct engines by fashioning metal. The Industrial Revolution was largely made possible by the invention of machine tools, machines, in other words, that were designed with the sole purpose of constructing other machines.

Nevertheless, those devices that build other devices are not exactly the kind of machine tools which Prime Minister Disraeli had in mind.

Since 1948, mathematicians have dreamed of building computers which were, so to speak, capable of becoming pregnant: they could be programmed to build replicas of themselves, and the replicas themselves could produce replicas, and so on, without limit. For in that year, the great American mathematician John von Neumann, in a lecture entitled 'The General and Logical Theory of Automata', laid down the principles of how such a feat could be achieved.[1]

The logical procedure suggested by von Neumann for constructing machines that would have the reproductive capacity of living organisms was at first regarded rather as a speculative mathematical curiosity – especially since the computers of his day were giants of 30 tons or more, and were little more than high-speed calculating devices.[2]

How could a machine be made to produce a copy of itself? The one way it *cannot* be made to do so is by receiving the order from its human programmer: 'Reproduce yourself.' For the machine can only reply in effect: 'I cannot reproduce myself, since I do not know who or what I am.' This approach would be as absurd as if a man were to give his wife a collection of bottles and flasks and ask her to build a baby. Instead, in von Neumann's view, the controlling human programmer should perform three simple actions when he sets out to create a dynasty of machines:

1 He gives the machine a complete description of itself.
2 He then gives the machine a second description of itself, *but this second description is of a machine which has already received the first description.*
3 Finally, he orders the machine to create another machine which corresponds precisely to the machine of the second description, and he orders the first machine to copy and pass on this final order to the second machine.

The most remarkable aspect of this sequence (which is much simpler than it may sound) is von Neumann's insight into the way in which living creatures reproduce. Five years after his lecture, in 1953, his ideas were confirmed when the biologists Francis Crick and James D. Watson cracked the genetic code and discovered the secret of organic reproduction.[3] It turned out to be essentially the same as the sequence for machine reproduction proposed by John von Neumann! Briefly, in living beings, the deoxyribonucleic acid (DNA), of which the cell is made, performs the role of the first machine. It gives instructions for the building of proteins to the substance ribonucleic acid (RNA), with which DNA is mixed, and which has been called its 'junior assistant'. While

RNA gets on with the somewhat dull task of building proteins for its parent organism and its offspring, DNA does the brilliant and imaginative work of programming its genes, which, in the case of a human baby, will decide whether its hair will be fair or dark, and whether its temperament will be excitable or phlegmatic.* In short, DNA and RNA together perform all the tasks which von Neumann's first machine must carry out in creating the second machine of the dynasty. And so, if we decide to construct self-reproducing machines, there is important *biological* evidence that von Neumann, long ago, hit upon the correct procedure for going about it.[4]

But why, it will be asked, should anyone *want* to build computers that constructed replicas of themselves? At best the procedure might be rather inconvenient. One could go to bed after an evening's work on the computer, come down the next morning, and find that instead of there being one computer there were two. What would these regenerative computers be for? The answer is that they will be used in far-off places to do difficult and dangerous jobs which people cannot easily perform.

The location of these places should be carefully considered. What is holding back our growth in technology? Why, more than ten years after men first walked on the Moon, is there still no permanent lunar colony? It has been more than three-quarters of a century since the first powered flight, and still the majority of human beings are confined to the surface of the Earth. Why?

The astronomer Frank J. Tipler, of the University of California at Berkeley, answered this question plainly in 1980 when he declared: 'It is a deficiency in computer tech-

---

*I am of course using hyperbole when attributing 'brilliance and imagination' to DNA. But the programming of genetic information is such a richly complex operation that the hyperbole seems justified.

nology, not in rocket technology, which prevents us from beginning the exploration of the Galaxy tomorrow.'[5] It is in space, not on Earth, that super-intelligent self-reproducing machines will come into their own; and it is in space that humanity's long-term future lies. It is fascinating to consider how Tipler and others who have looked into the far future see the way in which von Neumann machines will make possible, first the colonisation of our Solar System of planets, and then of our Milky Way Galaxy of more than 150,000 million suns.

14

Star-hopping

The vast expanses of the Pacific and Indian Oceans contain some quarter of a million habitable islands. They range from the countless tiny atolls of Micronesia and Polynesia to the land masses of Madagascar and Borneo. They fill an area, stretching from west to east from Africa to South America, and from north to south between Hawaii and New Zealand, of some 65 million square miles, one-third of the surface area of the globe.

So huge is this region that one might expect humanity to have taken hundreds of thousands of years to explore it and plant colonies wherever sources of fresh water could be found. But this was not the case. The main era of exploration and settlement, undertaken entirely by primitive peoples, took place within a mere 2,500 years.[1]

The peopling of these two mighty oceans, the greatest feat of maritime colonisation in history, was made possible by an ancient form of von Neumann machine: the double canoe. Imagine twin hulls about thirty feet in length, covered by a single deck, and with a lateen sail, a craft of similar design to a modern catamaran. These simple but rapid vessels, which may have averaged about twelve knots in a favourable wind, could have traversed distances of 2,000 miles in less than a week, making possible the settlement of islands at the rate of more than a hundred a year.*

These ships played the same role in the exploration of the

*Such boats were still being constructed at the time of Captain Cook's Pacific voyage in 1773. The above description is based on a sketch by one of his officers.

oceans as von Neumann machines will one day play in colonisation of the stars in the heavens. For they were self-reproducing in the sense that they were built wholly from local materials. Soon after an island was settled, fresh probes would be sent out to explore the neighbouring islands, carrying, as before, up to fifty passengers and crewmen and the food plants and domestic animals necessary for colonisation. The new island settlements provided starting points for fresh voyages of discovery, and so on, until every available niche in the two oceans had been filled by humanity – long before the arrival of settlers from Europe.

This tremendous achievement is likely to be repeated on a galactic scale. Indeed, a close analogy may be drawn between the historic method of settlement of hundreds of thousands of ocean islands and that of the tens of millions of habitable worlds likely to be in orbit round other stars. Just as the voyage of a single ship to a single island opened up a dozen more islands for colonisation, so the landing on one planet of a single automated probe will make possible the exploration of many other worlds at a speed immeasurably faster than human astronauts could accomplish the same feat.

One of the most important instruments carried within an intelligent, self-producing von Neumann machine will be a built-in spectrograph; a simple device, used today in landings on Mars and Venus, that analyses the chemical composition of the raw materials around its landing site. This ability to analyse extraterrestrial raw materials in a relatively 'stupid' machine, like the 1977 Viking Mars lander, would lead to vast possibilities in a more intelligent device that was able to act on its discoveries. In the words of the American scientist Theodore Taylor:

It is possible to imagine a machine that could scoop up material rocks from the Moon or rocks from asteroids – process them inside and make just about any product:

washing machines or teacups or automobiles or starships
... Once such a machine exists, it could gather sunlight
and the materials it is sitting on and produce on call
whatever products anybody wants.[2]

With this understanding, let us move now to what the
mathematician Frank J. Tipler, of the University of Texas
at Austin, calls the General Theory of Space Exploration
and Colonisation.[3] Professor Tipler's approach is startling
and original. Too many writers on interstellar travel today
still restrict themselves to calculations of how long it would
take to reach the nearest star, then multiply the answer to
this sum by a factor of thousands of millions, and gloomily
conclude that the colonisation of our Milky Way Galaxy of
more than 150,000 million suns is a feat likely to be forever
beyond the reach of man.

But Tipler, using the analogy of ocean island colonisation
and the coming availability of von Neumann machines,
makes the key point that once such a machine has been sent
to another solar system, *then the entire resources of that solar
system become available to the people who sent it*. Planets,
moons, asteroids and comets – all will be mined by the
machine for the construction of bases and factories to await
the arrival of human settlers. Work that would take many
centuries if done by humans will be accomplished within
months. Otherwise useless extraterrestrial materials, water,
hydrocarbons, nitrogen compounds, iron and nickel, and
other debris left over from the formation of distant suns,
can be made to pay for the entire cost of the project.

Yet the construction of bases and factories on alien worlds
will be but a prologue to the real task of the machine. This
will be to use those same extraterrestrial materials to construct hundreds of copies of itself, hundreds more von Neumann machines, which will set out on fresh expeditions
under their own, self-constructed, rocket propulsion, to do
the same work in hundreds of neighbouring solar systems.

On each of them, in turn, fresh bases and factories will be constructed; and from each of them, in turn, fresh von Neumann machines will be sent forth. And unlike the ocean explorers, who had no means of sending or receiving messages beyond their horizons, and who were therefore compelled to colonise *at random*, the von Neumann probes will be able to use radio messages to determine which stars have already been colonised by other probes.[4] What began as a single automated probe sent out from the neighbourhood of Earth becomes, *at no additional cost*, millions of probes criss-crossing the Galaxy, each doing the same work as the original parent device. At this rate, with each successful landing giving rise to hundreds of new ones, the entire Galaxy could be colonised – or at least made ready for colonisation – within about five million years; and all this great project of settlement would be made possible by a single machine!

On the political and social level, this scenario seems much more likely than the thousand-year investment plans hitherto envisaged, which the governments of Earth would review every few years and strike from their budgets whenever economy cuts were demanded. For this objection does not apply to von Neumann probes. As Tipler remarks, 'It is only necessary for societies to be motivated for interstellar exploration for the few years required to build the probe.' Once the machine had set forth, assuming there were no undetected or uncorrectable errors in its program, then no subsequent budget cuts, no loss of interest in it by public opinion, could prevent it from carrying out its mission. It would act on its own and it would pay its own way.

It is almost a cliché among writers about starships that several centuries must elapse before anything worthwhile can happen. By the standard of today's technology they are right. Most experts agree, rightly, that before *people* can travel to the stars, an automated probe must precede them to their destined solar system and send back information about the conditions it finds there. So much is obvious. It would be reckless to neglect such a precaution. The Apollo Moon-landing, for example, might never have been permitted had not the unmanned Surveyor probe first been sent to ascertain that the Lunar surface was stable, and did not consist of soft sand into which men and machines would sink without hope of rescue, as some astronomers feared.

But in the future, it will be seen as far too modest an aim to build a probe that merely sends back information. It is reasonable to assume that a von Neumann machine could do anything in months that humans could do in centuries or millennia. It would not only find out whether conditions were safe for human occupation; if they were not safe, it would make them safe. If the climate of an otherwise habitable planet was unsuitable, it would change the climate.* If dangerous alien life was present, the machine would eliminate it. If the raw materials for priceless hydrocarbon industrial fuels were locked up in the atmospheres of giant gas planets, alien versions of Jupiter and Saturn, it would extract them, making them ready for human use. If starfaring peoples had a taste for luxuries, then, on arriving on planets never previously visited, they would find whatever they desired. All these things the machine could do if it had been programmed to do them.

The only reason why we cannot begin this great project today is that nobody has yet succeeded in building a von Neumann machine. Yet judging by the present progress of computing, it is a reasonable assumption that such a machine could be built fairly early in the twenty-first century.

*Several methods have been proposed for 'terra-forming' planets even in our own solar system. Carl Sagan, for example, has proposed breaking down the unbreathable carbon dioxide atmosphere of the planet Venus into oxygen and carbon, by the introduction of algae micro-organisms. For a full description of this idea, see Chapters 6 and 7 of my book *The Next Ten Thousand Years* (Cape, 1974).

Allowing another few decades for programming and testing it and making improvements, it could be launched towards one of the nearest stars by the middle of the next century. Even by the present level of chemical rocket technology, it could leave the Solar System at a speed of 40,000 m.p.h., the cruising velocity of the American Voyager spacecraft that have visited Jupiter and Saturn. This speed could be more than quadrupled to 200,000 m.p.h. by using Jupiter's gravitational field as an accelerator.

But these rocket engines will be as nothing to those likely to be available within a century. The unmanned Daedalus starship, proposed in 1978 by the British Interplanetary Society, would be propelled by the continuous explosions of miniature hydrogen bombs at the rate of 250 detonations per second, and would have a cruising velocity of 80 million m.p.h., just under 12 per cent of the speed of light.[5] The journey of the von Neumann machine to the nearest star, Proxima Centauri, which is 4·3 light-years distant,* could therefore be accomplished in differing voyage-times, depending on the type of rocket used:

Table 3

Cruising speed (m.p.h.)	Voyage-time (years)
40,000	72,000
200,000	15,000
80,000,000	36

A voyage-time of 36 years – if it is permissible to extrapolate to a rocket technology which appears perfectly feasible on paper, but which does not yet exist – would be followed by an epoch in which innumerable interstellar voyages were taking place simultaneously. The great project of galactic

*A light-year, a common unit in astronomy for measuring distances, is the distance light travels in a year, moving at its constant speed of 670 million m.p.h. It is about six trillion miles.

colonisation would have begun, paying its own costs in their entirety. The first von Neumann machine would carry its own empire-building equipment in electronic software. It would start to transform the Universe, just as the first double canoe that set forth so many thousands of years ago started to transform the oceans.

15

The End of Time

CASSIUS:
How many ages hence
Shall this our lofty scene be acted o'er,
In states unborn and accents yet unknown!
Julius Caesar, III. i. 111–13

Will time end, or will it go on for ever? This strange-seeming question that now so perplexes astronomers will, when answered definitively, indicate more clearly the ultimate destiny of thinking beings. And by 'thinking beings', I mean thinking machines, whose rugged physical natures will surely make them the ultimate inheritors of the Universe.

The question at first sight appears to have no meaning, since 'time' is generally regarded as an abstract thing, which cannot be said to 'end' or 'begin'.

Yet this is not the case. All our present knowledge of the state of the Universe, based on Einstein's 1916 general theory of relativity, predicts that there must have been a single beginning of everything, that matter, space and time came into existence simultaneously in a primordial explosion called the Big Bang, some 20,000 million years ago.

This idea must be explained in a little more detail, so that what follows will be intelligible. It is often asked, what happened *before* the Big Bang? The question is meaningless. There was no 'before', since the Big Bang marked the beginning of time. And again, some people ask, where did the Big Bang happen? But again the question has no meaning, for the Big Bang created all the space that now exists. In short, it happened everywhere.

143

What had a beginning may surely have an end; and if man is ultimately to be succeeded by super-intelligent machines, as appears likely, then the machines themselves will be in a position to influence the nature of the end of time.

The previous chapter discussed events that may take place millions, or perhaps tens of millions, of years hence. But we must now turn our attention to a future incomparably more remote – not of tens of millions, but of tens of *billions* of years, when the Universe, and everything in it, may be approaching its end.*

As far as astronomers and physicists now understand the matter, there are only two ways in which the end of the Universe will come. If the total weight, or 'mass', of the Universe exceeds a certain critical limit, then all the galaxies – giant groups of stars like our own Milky Way – which are still rushing apart from each other under the original impetus of the Big Bang, will eventually halt their expansion. Overwhelmed by the force of gravity, they will rush together, collapsing into a single object of infinitesimal size and infinite density that retains all its original mass. This event, the so-called Big Crunch, will, if it occurs, start to happen within about 50,000 million years.

If, on the other hand, the mass of the Universe is *below* that critical limit – and there is yet no consensus on the question – then the galaxies will continue to rush apart from each other for eternity. Life and energy will die, but of space and time there will be no end.

The question must now be asked: which kind of Universe would we *prefer* to be living in, a 'closed' collapsing Universe, or an 'open', ever-expanding one with an unimaginably longer life-span, but which eventually 'dies' for all practical purposes from the exhaustion of its nuclear fuel?

The question indeed seems preposterous in the twentieth century, because there is nothing we can do about it, and most people do not trouble themselves about what may or

*By 'billion', I mean 1,000 million.

may not happen in 50 billion years' time. Even scientists who write about the beginnings of the Universe with the utmost seriousness adopt an almost apologetic or jocular tone when they discuss its end, as if they feared ridicule.[1] In the words of one of them: 'The study of the remote future still seems to be as disreputable today as the study of the remote past was thirty years ago.'[2] For surely the question is academic. How can intellect be expected to survive when the stars lose their warmth? To Jamal N. Islam, of University College, Cardiff, the prospect is fanciful:

> It seems unlikely that civilisation in any form can survive indefinitely, even if it were socially able to do so, and even if its technology could be developed to the theoretical limits. No new forms of life can be developed once the Universe becomes sufficiently cold.[3]

It is with this prediction that we shall presently be taking issue.

Consider that figure of 'about 50,000 million years' between now and the possible Big Crunch. It seems an enormous amount of time, but it is nothing compared with the number that is now to follow. The number of billionths of a second in 50 billion years is but a tiny, imperceptible fraction of Freeman Dyson's Number, the number of years in which, according to the calculation of Freeman J. Dyson of the Institute for Advanced Study at Princeton, intelligent life will be possible in an ever-expanding Universe whose mass is below the critical limit that would bring about gravitational collapse.[4]

If very large numbers are held to be repellent, then Freeman Dyson's Number is a truly horrible statistic! Before all the nuclear fuel in the Universe is exhausted, before all the stars have died – and before the deaths of all the shining stars that have yet to shine, through countless billions of generations of shining stars, then, before the whole Universe turns black, the number of years that will have elapsed will be 10 to the power of 10 to the power of 76.

The enormity of this number may be shown by the position of the parentheses which Dyson has assigned to it. They go on the upper two figures, so that it reads: 10 to the power of (10 raised to the power of 76).*

No pocket calculator can handle a number so vast. Indeed, even to write the number down in the ordinary way, without using that convenient shorthand phrase 'to the power of', presents great difficulties. If one were to start with a 1 and then add all the necessary zeros, and if each digit was no larger than a hydrogen atom, and if one were to write down digits at the rate of 1,000 billion every second, then one would need no fewer than 200,000 *billion billion billion billion* planets the size of the Earth upon whose surface to write down the number. Nor would the task of writing it be a mere afternoon's amusement, even with instant and simultaneous access to all those innumerable planets. The sheer task of writing it, even in these vastly accelerated conditions, would take approximately 3,000 billion billion billion billion billion billion billion billion years, that is, 3 followed by sixty-six zeros. [5]

This, when trillionths of a second have been replaced by years, is the amount of time, according to Dyson's calculation, which will be available to intelligent beings in the event of an open, ever-expanding Universe – before the relics of the stars-that-have-yet-to-be have collapsed into dark ruin and emit no more radiation. The question, therefore, of which kind of ultimate fate *we would prefer* has answered itself. What we, in the twentieth century, might casually think of such a question has no importance or interest whatsoever; but to the descendants of the von Neumann machines towards whose construction we are now groping, it will be an issue transcending all others.

*Parentheses placed differently would produce a much lower number, a 'mere' 1 followed by 760 zeros.

Suppose [says Dyson] that we discover this Universe to be naturally closed and doomed to collapse. Is it conceivable that by intelligent intervention, converting matter into radiation, and causing matter to flow purposefully on a cosmic scale, we could break open a closed Universe and change the topology of space-time so that only a part of it would collapse and another part of it would expand for ever? ... If it turns out that the Universe is closed, then we shall still have about 10,000 million years to explore the possibility of a technological fix that would burst it open.[6]

It would take a bold science-fiction writer indeed to suggest that mankind could ever undertake such a task. For the 'technological fix' envisioned by Dyson involves nothing less than the physical manipulation of billions of galaxies each about 100 billion times more massive than the Sun, and forcing them to travel in the opposite direction to that in which they might be falling already, thereby halting the collapse and averting the Big Crunch.

But a dynasty of machines could do what humanity could not. Unlike people, they would be virtually immortal; when they found themselves wearing out, it would be a simple matter for them to replace their ailing parts with the metallic debris of long-broken worlds. To such beings, a billion years might be as yesterday. They could redesign themselves as they found necessary. They could grow in mass and strength until the most powerfully exploding objects were insignificant things by comparison. With the ability to construct their own internal power systems, they could make themselves impervious to heat or cold. They would function without needing the warming radiance of the stars. Here is the answer to the objection raised by Jamal Islam that '*No new forms of life can be developed once the Universe becomes sufficiently cold.*' For billions of years will be available in which to design themselves for the purpose of cosmic

147

reconstruction, as Dyson has pointed out. Biological creatures need external warmth, but machines such as these will not.

It is hard to imagine the nature of such god-like creatures, even though, in a sense, they will be our descendants. But one sure prediction can be made about their behaviour. Like all thinking entities, they will have the will to survive. And survival, to them, will mean one thing only: preventing the Universe from collapsing into a black hole, into the Big Crunch, in which even they could no longer function, for space and time would be no more.

What then could they do to prevent this catastrophe? They might, as Dyson suggests, find some means of converting matter into radiation and thus reduce that dangerous gravitational attraction that matter extends towards matter. Or, if this approach was not practical, or carried with it some undesired side-effects, they might prepare monstrous explosions to force the galaxies to move in more convenient directions. Even today, glancing at astronomical photographs, one can imagine what such an engineering enterprise would look like from afar. The galaxy Messier 87, in the constellation of Virgo, has shot out into space a titanic flare, a jet of brightness nearly 100,000 light-years in length.[7] One might imagine (although there is not the slightest evidence to support such a suggestion), that some vastly powerful machine civilisation is even now using this jet for some purpose of its own. The jet is in all probability the result of some natural explosion; but one cannot help remarking on the likelihood that Messier 87 *is actually being moved by it*, in accordance with Isaac Newton's Third Law that every action has its equal and opposite reaction.

It is possible that other biological civilisations in the cosmos have invented space-faring von Neumann machines, or that plans have been laid for the construction of their even more advanced successors. Possible, perhaps, but not very likely. For any other intelligent civilisation in our own, local Milky Way would surely by now have colonised every habitable system. It is self-evident that they have not done so. No little green men seem to have reached the Earth, either now or in prehistoric times. This fact has led an increasing number of astronomers to conclude, not that the project of galactic colonisation is impossible, but that in our Galaxy at least, other technical civilisations do not exist.[8]

The human race and its successors will inherit the heavens. The development of computers begun in this century will open up realms beyond the dream of Cassius which opens this chapter. Let me conclude by quoting Dyson once more:[9]

> If my view of the future is correct, it means that the world of physics and astronomy is inexhaustible. No matter how far we look into the future, there will always be new things happening, new information coming in, new worlds to explore, a constantly expanding domain of life, consciousness and memory.

Glossary

Algorithm. A step by step method of using programming to solve a problem.

Artificial intelligence. The science, or art, of teaching machines how to think.

Artificial paranoia. A program designed to make a machine think it is being persecuted.

Basic. An acronym for Beginners' All-purpose Symbolic Instruction Code, the most commonly used programming language; limited in scope but very easy to learn.

Bug. An error in a program.

Byte. The amount of memory space filled by each of the single characters, or letters, in a computer program. The command PRINT"HAPPY", for example, occupies twelve bytes.

Cassette drive. A tape recorder attached to a computer which stores programs. See also *Floppy disk drive.*

Central processing unit. The central part of the computer's 'brain', also called the microprocessor.

Chip. A tiny component, made mostly of silicon, containing pre-programmed instructions, one or more of which make up the inner parts of a microcomputer.

Crash. The breakdown of a computer program.

Cursor. The flashing spot on a computer's screen which acts as a marker.

Expert system. A program devoted to knowledge of one subject and able to explain its own reasoning.

Floppy disk (operated by a *floppy disk drive*). A medium the size of a small gramophone record, for storing programs.

Floppy disk drive. A machine which processes the contents

of floppy disks. It is used for recording programs and feeding them into the computer.

Flowchart. A plan, usually a diagram, which shows how a program is designed to operate.

Hacker. A person obsessed with programming.

Hardware. The engineered parts of a machine, as opposed to the software, or program.

Input. Material entered into the computer by its user.

List. An instruction to a computer to display its program.

Lovelace regime. The belief, widely held before 1960, that a computer could be only an obedient slave. It was overthrown by the discovery that games-playing programs could defeat their own creators.

Machine. A term with many definitions. Here is mine: a device which operates independently of biological muscle-power.

Machine code. The language in which the computer actually operates. It is one of the most difficult to write. It can act upon commands many times faster than Basic.

Mainframe computer. A large and powerful computer, which often requires a considerable supervisory staff. The functions of these very expensive machines are being rapidly superseded by much smaller and cheaper machines.

Mainframe flat-earther. A person who believes, wrongly, that computers other than mainframes are useless, or mere toys.

Microcomputer. A desk-top computer, costing only a few hundred pounds or dollars, with some of the power and sophistication of some of the more old-fashioned mainframes.

Microprocessor. See *Central processing unit*.

Pattern recognition. The ability of a computer to recognise visually or by other senses.

Peripheral. An extra device attached to a computer, such as a *cassette drive* or a printer.

Plug. The main power source of a machine. There is a belief that if the machine gets out of control, 'We can always pull out the plug.' But in a sufficiently powerful and intelligent machine this is unlikely to be true, for the machine may itself find an alternative power source.

Print. A command, in Basic, which tells a computer which words to display on its screen or transmit to a printer.

Program. A set of instructions which tells a computer what to do.

Programmer. A person who writes programs.

Programming language. The language in which a program is written. There are thousands of such languages, with names like Pascal, Cobol, Lisp, etc., since each main language has innumerable dialects.

Random Access Memory, abbreviated RAM. The memory in a computer available to humans for writing programs and storing data.

Read Only Memory, abbreviated ROM. The memory a computer uses for its permanent, unchangeable instructions.

Robot. A mechanical worker, usually in a factory, which may be controlled by a computer.

Robotics. The study or creation of robots.

Subroutine. A set of instructions that appear only once in a program, but which can be executed many times.

System. A term with two meanings: the way in which a computer and its peripherals are arranged, or the interconnection of several computers.

Terminal. A screen and keyboard connected to a computer. A computer can have many terminals, even in different parts of the world.

Time-sharing. Two or more people operating a computer through different terminals.

Tree. A large range of possibilities in a complex program, which the computer must analyse, usually one at a time.

Turing Test. A test devised by the mathematician Alan Turing to discover whether a machine is 'intelligent'.

Von Neumann machine. A machine which could produce an exact copy of itself.

Notes and References

N.B. Where publication details of books cited are not given below, please see Bibliography.

Introduction

1 Quoted by Robert Jastrow in 'Our Brain's Successor', *Science Digest*, vol. 89, no. 2, March 1981.
2 'Welcome the Big Boys', editorial in *Practical Computing*, vol. 4, no. 12, December 1981.
3 Using such programs as Visicalc and, for more advanced analysis, 'expert systems'. For an account of these see Chapter 8.

1 Real and Faked Intelligence

1 R. P. Abelson, 'The Structure of Belief Systems', a contribution to *Computer Models of Thought and Language* by Kenneth Colby and Roger Schank (eds). See also Chapter 4 of Margaret Boden's *Artificial Intelligence and Natural Man*. It is interesting that Abelson chose Mr Goldwater for his electronic mimicry for the same reason as I chose Mr Wedgwood Benn, because his ideology (as expressed in his speeches) 'is relatively clear and self-consistent'.
2 A. Berry, 'Switch on your own Politician', *Daily Telegraph*, 5 December 1980.
3 A. M. Turing, 'Computing Machinery and Intelligence', *Mind: A Quarterly Review of Psychology and Philosophy*, vol. 59, p. 236, October 1950. This classic paper has been reprinted many times: for example, in J. Mack Adams and Douglas H. Haden (eds), *Social Effects of Computer Use and Misuse*; and in *Creative Computing*, vol. 6, pp. 44–53, January 1980.
4 G. Jefferson, 'The Mind of Mechanical Man' (Lister Oration for 1949), *British Medical Journal*, vol. 1, pp. 1105–21, 1949.

2 *The Turing Test*

1 A. M. Turing, 'Computing Machinery and Intelligence', *Mind: A Quarterly Review of Psychology and Philosophy*, vol. 59, p. 236, October 1950.

2 Perhaps the existence of an afterlife may eventually be settled by scientific experiment. In the United States there is an organisation, known as the Association for the Scientific Study of Near-Death Phenomena, which collects case-studies of people who have been pronounced 'clinically dead' and have then unexpectedly recovered. The idea is that since, for a moment, they were technically dead, they are able to give accurate reports of what death was like. See D. Ingber, 'Vision of an Afterlife', *Science Digest*, vol. 89, no. 1, January–February 1981; also, A. Berry, 'Seeking Evidence of an Afterlife', *Daily Telegraph*, 12 January 1981.

3 D. Levy, 'Computers are now Chess Masters', *New Scientist*, vol. 79, no. 1113, pp. 256–8, 27 July 1978; also, ibid., 'Levy beats Chess-Playing Computer', p. 75, 14 September 1978.

4 For an account of this match (played in Monte Carlo in 1979), which was a sensational development in artificial intelligence, see H. Berliner, 'Computer Backgammon', *Scientific American*, vol. 242, no. 6, pp. 64–72, June 1980.

5 A point made forcefully by Robert Jastrow, in his article 'Our Brain's Successor', *Science Digest*, vol. 89, no. 2, March 1981.

3 *The Fall of the Lovelace Regime*

1 Margaret Boden, *Artificial Intelligence and Natural Man*, p. 419.

2 G. Robinson, 'How to Tell Your Friends from Machines', *Mind: A Quarterly Review of Psychology and Philosophy*, vol. 81, no. 324, pp. 504–18, October 1972.

3 Joseph Weizenbaum, *Computer Power and Human Reason*. Despite these polemics, this is a valuable book which says a great deal about artificial intelligence before coming to the conclusion that it is thoroughly evil.

4 From the short story 'Answer', in *The Best of Frederic Browne*, Ballantine Books, New York, 1977.

5 From the short story 'Moxon's Master', in *The Collected Writings of Ambrose Bierce*, Citadel Press, New York, 1970.

6 See, for example, Jerry M. Rosenberg, *The Computer Prophets*.

7 The world's fastest and most powerful operating computer (1982) is the Cray-1, with 8,388,608 bytes of memory storage capacity, designed by Seymour R. Cray, of Cray Research Inc., Minneapolis. In 1979, its price was quoted at about $8·8 million.

8 Christopher Evans, *The Mighty Micro*, p. 170.

9 Ada, Countess of Lovelace, *Observations on Mr. Babbage's Analytical Engine*, quoted in ibid., p. 27.

10 H. Berliner, 'Computer Backgammon', *Scientific American*, vol. 242, no. 6, pp. 64–72, June 1980. The point about the ultimate social usefulness of computer games programs is also emphasised in Eliot Hearst's contribution to *Chess Skill in Man and Machine* by Peter W. Frey (ed.), pp. 168–70.

11 A. Newall, J. Shaw and H. Simon, 'Chess-Playing Programs and the Problem of Complexity', *IBM Journal of Research and Development*, vol. 2, pp. 320–35, 1958.

12 E. Fredkin, 'Long Range Prospects for Intelligence Information Processing', paper completed in May 1979 and kindly furnished by its author.

13 Arthur C. Clarke, private communication.

4 Thirty Hours at the Console

1 Stanley Greenblatt, *Understanding Computers Through Common Sense*.

2 See, for example, I. Asimov, 'I Robot', *The Rest of the Robots*, Panther, London, 1968.

3 ibid.

4 From Joseph Weizenbaum, *Computer Power and Human Reason*.

5 If, Then . . .

1 King James IV of Scotland, reigned 1473–1513. See the *Dictionary of National Biography*, Oxford University Press, 1908, vol. 10, pp. 582–90.

2 *Richard III*, III. i. 169–78.

3 ibid., III. i. 181–3.

4 ibid., III. i. 191–3.

5 Stanley Greenblatt, in Chapter 2 of *Understanding Computers Through Common Sense*.

6 From 'Paul Revere's Ride', in *The Later Poems of Henry Wadsworth Longfellow*, Bell and Daldy, London, 1866.

7 Encyclopaedia-type programs, of the kind described here but containing far more information, could be used in a computer

program to classify the kings and queens of England, American presidents, football, baseball or cricket players, or any other field where information can be stored in entries.

6 The Machine That Was Hunted by the Mafia

1 Kenneth Colby, *Artificial Paranoia*. See also, K. M. Colby, S. Weber and F. D. Hilf, 'Artificial Paranoia', *Artificial Intelligence*, vol. 2, pp. 1–25, 1971. 'Parry' is a 35,000-byte program, of which 14,000 bytes make up its data-base. It was written by Colby and his team as part of the continuing Stanford University Artificial Intelligence Project in the high-level programming languages LISP and MLISP.

2 Colby, *Artificial Paranoia*, p. 2.

3 ibid., p. 43.

4 Colby, Weber and Hilf, op. cit., pp. 16–18.

5 ibid., pp. 19–20.

6 See, for example, Carl Rogers, *Counselling and Psychotherapy*, Houghton Mifflin, Boston, 1942.

7 Joseph Weizenbaum, *Computer Power and Human Reason*, pp. 3–4.

8 A tape cassette published in 1978 by Petsoft, Birmingham.

9 Weizenbaum, op. cit., pp. 6–7.

10 Quoted by Margaret Boden in *Artificial Intelligence and Natural Man*, p. 96; see also Steven Kaneff (ed.), *Picture Language Machines*, Academic Press, New York, 1970, pp. 32–3. I had a similarly curious conversation with Eliza which increased my sympathy for the vice-president:

Can I use the computer this morning?
PERHAPS YOU DON'T WANT TO USE THE COMPUTER THIS MORNING?
I most certainly do. Can I use it?
DO YOU WANT TO BE ABLE TO USE THE COMPUTER?
Can I use it?
PERHAPS YOU DON'T WANT TO USE IT?
I do. Is it all right if I use it?
SAY, DO YOU HAVE ANY PSYCHOLOGICAL PROBLEMS?

11 Terry Winograd, *Understanding Natural Language*, pp. 8–15.

For interesting comments on this dialogue, see also Boden, op. cit., pp. 115–22.
12 Boden, op. cit., pp. 123–4.

7 *Shots Were Heard in the Embassy!*

1 R. C. Schank, 'Interestingness: Controlling Inferences', *Artificial Intelligence*, vol. 12, pp. 273–97, 1979.
2 ibid.
3 ibid.
4 Margaret Boden, *Artificial Intelligence and Natural Man*, p. 112. Terry Winograd compared the following two sentences:
A. The city councillors refused to give the women a permit for a demonstration because they feared violence.
B. The city council refused to give the women a permit for a demonstration because they advocated revolution.
   The decision to ascribe 'they' to the councillors in the first sentence, and 'they' to the women in the second – if a machine could be taught to make this differentiation – would imply a network of knowledge of social and political life. See Terry Winograd, *Understanding Natural Language*. Quoted by D. Michie, 'Machine and the Theory of Intelligence', *Nature*, vol. 241, 23 February 1973.
5 R. Wilensky, 'Understanding Goal-Based Stories', Yale University Department of Computer Science, research report 140, September 1978.
6 These conversations are reported in ibid., pp. 4–5.
7 Gerard Francis Dejong, 'Skimming Stories in Real Time: An Experiment in Integrated Understanding', Yale University Department of Computer Science, research report 158, May 1979.
8 ibid., p. 27.
9 ibid., pp. 167–70. It is only fair to add that when a slight improvement had been added to Frump's education, when it had been told that the mere 'testing' of a bomb was not necessarily a hostile act, the next time it got the story right: 'LEONID BREZHNEV TOLD THE UNITED STATES THAT RUSSIA HAD TESTED A BOMB.'
10 ibid., pp. 173–4.
11 Boden, op. cit., p. 299.
12 James R. Meehan, 'The Metanovel: Writing Stories by Com-

puter', Yale University Department of Computer Science, research report 75, September 1976.

13 ibid., p. 51.
14 ibid., p. 127.
15 ibid., p. 37. It is fascinating to compare Tale-spin's version of 'The Fox and the Crow' with Aesop's subtler and less stilted original. This reads, in a translation by V. S. Vernon-Jones (*Aesop's Fables*, Heinemann, London, 1912):

> A Crow was sitting on a branch of a tree with a piece of cheese in her beak when a Fox observed her and set his wits to discover some way of getting the cheese. Coming and standing under the tree, he looked up and said: 'What a noble bird I see above me! Her beauty is without equal, the hue of her plumage exquisite. If only her voice is as sweet as her looks are fair, she ought without doubt to be Queen of Birds.' The Crow was hugely flattered by this, and just to show the Fox that she could sing she gave a loud caw. Down came the cheese, of course, and the Fox, snatching it up, said: 'You have a voice, madam, I see. What you want is wits.'

16 ibid., pp. 228–30.

8 *Victory by Espionage*

1 Peter W. Frey, *Chess Skill in Man and Machine*, p. 36.
2 A. D. de Groot and R. W. Jongman, 'Heuristics in Perceptual Processes', a paper presented to the 1966 International Congress of Psychology in Moscow. Quoted in Frey, op. cit., p. 36. See also de Groot, *Thought and Choice in Chess*, Mouton, The Hague, 1965. Those further interested in the fascinating subject of chess-playing machines should look at Dave and Kathe Spracklens' *Sargon: A Computer Chess Program*. T. A. Marsland's 'Bibliography of computer chess', *Machine Intelligence*, vol. 9, pp. 385–403, 1979, lists the 332 papers that have been written on the subject up to mid-1978 or thereabouts.
3 D. Levy, 'Are Game-Playing Programs Intelligent?' *Computer Age*, December 1979.
4 See, for example, R. C. Schank and J. Kolodner, 'Retrieving Information from an Episodic Memory – or, Why Computers' Memories Should Be More Like People's', Yale

University Department of Computer Science, research report 159, January 1979.

5 Professor B. Raphael, *The Thinking Computer*, p. 78. The word 'cheat' is my own interpretation of Raphael's argument. In a game, to seek help from a third party would of course be cheating, but in love, war or treasure-hunting all is fair.

6 From *The Works of Edgar Allan Poe*, vol. 3, The Colonial Company, New York and Pittsburg, 1894.

7 Kubrick, quoted in Humphrey Walwyn's article, 'Computers in the Movies', *Microcomputer Printout*, vol. 3, no. 5, pp. 52–5, April 1982.

8 N. V. Findler, 'Computer Poker', *Scientific American*, vol. 239, no. 1, pp. 112–19, July 1978.

9 ibid.

10 For a general view of expert systems, and of the progress of machine learning to date, see D. Michie, 'Experiments on the Mechanisation of Game-Learning', *The Computer Journal*, vol. 25, no. 1, pp. 105–13, February 1982.

11 A. Berry, 'Computer Unravels Political Risk', *Daily Telegraph*, 26 February 1982.

9 *Camels, Weasels and Whales*

1 Predictions were made on these lines at the 1980 annual conference of the American Association for the Advancement of Science, in San Francisco, by Mr Gordon Moore, president of Intel Corporation, and Dr John Mayo, of Bell Telephone Laboratories, New Jersey.

2 'Pilots and Aircraft are on Speaking Terms', *New Scientist*, 18 September 1980.

3 There is a vast amount of literature on the skill of recognising faces and teaching that skill to a computer. See, for example, L. D. Harmon, 'The Recognition of Faces', *Scientific American*, vol. 229, pp. 70–82, November 1973; G. M. Davies, J. W. Shepherd and H. D. Ellis, 'Remembering Faces: Acknowledging our Limitations', *Journal of the Forensic Science Society*, vol. 18, pp. 19–24, 1978; I. Aleksander, 'Action-Oriented Learning Networks', *Kybernetes*, vol. 4, pp. 29–44, 1975; I. Aleksander and T. J. Stonham, 'Guide to Pattern Recognition using Random-Access Memories', *Computer and Digital Techniques*, vol. 2, no. 1, pp. 29–40, 1979; also, A. J. Goldstein, L. D. Harmon and A. B. Lesk, 'Identification of Human

Faces', *Proceedings of the IEEE*, vol. 59, no. 5, pp. 748–69, May 1971.

4 In 1971, Mr A. T. Lawton drew a binary-code picture of a suited astronaut on a rectangular grid of 59,200 squares. It would be accurate to say that it imparted $59,200 \div 81 = 731$ times more information than my swastika drawing! See Lawton, 'Startalk: the Problems of Interstellar Communication', *Spaceflight*, vol. 13, pp. 241–4, July 1971.

5 Davies, Shepherd and Ellis, op. cit.

6 S. Solomon, 'Miracle Workers', *Science Digest*, December 1981.

10   A Cacophony of Voices

1 Plato, in his *Phaedrus*, said there were two distinct kinds of oracular divination, the 'sane' and the 'insane'. In the former, the priests and priestesses were calm and logical, and in the latter 'enthusiastic', 'ecstatic' or 'possessed'. Robert Graves, in his novel *I Claudius*, puts into the mouth of the emperor the view that the 'inspired' priestesses of Apollo at Cumae 'seem more inspired by Bacchus than by Apollo, the drunken nonsense they deliver'.

2 See, for examples, the entry for 'Oracles' in the *Dictionary of Phrase and Fable*, ed. Brewer, Cassell, London, 1970.

3 ibid.

4 According to a report by Jelinek on 19 April 1980, to the American Society of Automotive Engineers, at Houston, Texas. *Daily Telegraph*, 21 April 1980.

5 A. Berry, 'Computer Sid learns to turn Deaf Ear', *Daily Telegraph*, 21 March 1981.

6 ibid.

7 An excellent survey of talking and listening machines appeared in the article 'Chatty Computers' by William M. Bulkeley, *Wall Street Journal*, 31 December 1980.

8 'Pilots and Aircraft are on Speaking Terms', *New Scientist*, 18 September 1980.

9 S. E. Levinson and M. Y. Liberman, 'Speech Recognition by Computer', *Scientific American*, vol. 244, pp. 64–76, April 1981.

10 ibid.

11 T. George, 'Jobs versus Micro-chips', *Electronics and Computing*, June 1981.

11 The Supercomputer

1 For details of the Cray 1, see note 7 to Chapter 3. The Cray 1 is soon to be exceeded in power and speed by a projected $50 million machine for use in NASA's Ames Research Center at Palo Alto, California.

2 In normal codes, where messages are translated into strings of digits, the sender must tell the recipient in advance what the key is; and at this point the code is vulnerable, since this preliminary message cannot be sent in code. But in the ingenious system devised by Martin Hellman and Whitfield Diffie, of Stanford University, California, and by Ronald Rivest, of the Massachusetts Institute of Technology, two complete strangers are able to communicate without previous contact – provided, of course, that they both possess powerful computing facilities.

In essence, it works like this. The would-be recipient of secret messages discovers a pair of prime numbers (prime numbers being infinite in number and divisible only by themselves and by 1). Each prime must be at least fifty digits in length. He then advertises his name and the *product* of these primes in a central 'directory'. The sender composes a message to him based on a numerical key of this gigantic prime product. The receiver alone can decode it, since only he can construct a numerical 'matrix' of the secret primes. The principle of the system is that *the world's most powerful computers cannot find the primes of a prime product in a period of less than several decades if the primes themselves have more than about fifty digits*. A full explanation of this system is given in Roger Rapoport's article 'Unbreakable Code', *Omni*, vol. 2, no. 12, September 1980. See also A. Berry, 'Tackling Codes', *Daily Telegraph*, 22 September 1980.

3 The likely construction of a Supercomputer is described in detail by J. Matisoo in 'The Superconducting Computer', *Scientific American*, vol. 242, no. 5, pp. 50–65, May 1980; also by J. E. Bishop in 'Can a Supercomputer be Built? Team at IBM grows more confident', *Wall Street Journal*, 27 February 1981. My description of the projected machine has been largely based on these two articles. Of additional interest on the subject of super-conducting materials and their applications is T. H. Geballe and J. K. Hulm, 'Superconductors in Electric-Power Technology', *Scientific American*, vol. 243, no. 5, pp. 138–72, November 1980.

12 *When You Can't Pull Out the Plug*

1 Roald Dahl, *Tales of the Unexpected*, Penguin Books, London, 1979.
2 For a good account of this new industrial technology, see Joseph F. Engelberger's *Robots in Practice: Management and Applications of Industrial Robots.*
3 H. Berliner, quoted in *Newsweek*, June 1980.
4 Frank George, *Machine Takeover*, Chapter 7.
5 ibid.
6 There is an excellent discussion of this point in Robert Jastrow's article 'The Post-Human World', *Science Digest*, vol. 89, no. 1, pp. 89–144, January–February 1981.
7 I have not mentioned that there is an intermediate state, very large-scale integration (VLSI), using submicron-sized circuits, now in imminent prospect of coming on to the market.
8 A good popular account of Heisenberg's Uncertainty Principle (although I say it myself!) is to be found in my book *From Apes to Astronauts*, pp. 116–18.
9 John Barker, of Warwick University, quoted in the *Daily Mail*, 14 November 1980. See also J. Barker, 'Now it's Smaller than Light', *Guardian*, 27 March 1980. I am most indebted to Dr Barker for showing me a copy of his unpublished paper, 'The Vanishing Transistor', written in March 1980.
10 E. Fredkin, quoted in Pamela McCorduck's *Machines Who Think*, p. 150.
11 I am indebted to A. T. Lawton for giving me the idea for this story.

13 *Von Neumann's Machines*

1 This famous lecture is reproduced on pp. 288–328 of von Neumann's *Collected Works*, Pergamon, Oxford, 1963.
2 The ENIAC Machine, built by von Neumann and his colleagues in the 1940s, weighed 30 tons and consumed 150,000 watts of electricity. By contrast, the most powerful microcomputer on the market in 1982 weighs about 50 lb and consumes only 50 watts. It also operates many thousands of times faster than ENIAC. This particular machine, the Commodore Business Machines' 'micro-mainframe computer', sells for about

$6,000 at the time of writing compared with a price of tens of millions of dollars for ENIAC.

3 This point was vividly made in Freeman J. Dyson's 'The Twenty-First Century', Vanuxem Lecture delivered at Princeton University, 26 February 1970.

4 A more complete description of this idea may be found in Chapter 11 of my book *The Next Ten Thousand Years*.

5 F. J. Tipler, 'Extraterrestrial Intelligent Beings Do Not Exist', *Quarterly Journal of the Royal Astronomical Society*, vol. 21, pp. 267–81, 1980. Contained in this paper, which deals mainly with the author's hypothesis that alien civilisations do not exist in our Galaxy, since their spacecraft seem never to have visited the Earth, is a detailed description of how *we* could colonise the Galaxy with von Neumann machines.

14 Star-hopping

1 See, for example, P. S. Bellwood, 'The Peopling of the Pacific', *Scientific American*, vol. 243, no. 5, pp. 174–85, November 1980; William Howells, *The Pacific Islanders*, Weidenfeld & Nicolson, London, 1973; R. H. MacArthur and E. O. Wilson, *The Theory of Island Biogeography*, Princeton University Press, New Jersey, 1967.

2 Theodore Taylor, quoted in Nigel Calder's *Spaceships of the Mind*, p. 18.

3 F. J. Tipler, 'Extraterrestrial Intelligent Beings Do Not Exist', *Quarterly Journal of the Royal Astronomical Society*, vol. 21, pp. 267–81, 1980.

4 Tipler, 'Additional Remarks on Extraterrestrial Intelligence', ibid., vol. 22, pp. 279–92, 1981.

5 *Project Daedalus*, British Interplanetary Society, London, 1978. See also, 'Cruising at 84 million m.p.h.', a chapter in my book *From Apes to Astronauts*.

15 The End of Time

1 See, for example, P. C. W. Davies, 'The Thermal Future of the Universe', *Monthly Notices of the Royal Astronomical Society*, vol. 161, pp. 1–5, 1973; J. D. Barrow and F. J. Tipler, 'Eternity is Unstable', *Nature*, vol. 276, 1978; M. J. Rees, 'The Collapse of the Universe: An Eschatological Study', the *Observatory*, vol. 89, pp. 193–8, October 1969; J. N. Islam, 'Possible Ulti-

mate Fate of the Universe', *Quarterly Journal of the Royal Astronomical Society*, vol. 18, pp. 3–8, 1977. See also Islam, 'The Ultimate Fate of the Universe', *Sky and Telescope*, vol. 57, pp. 13–18, January 1979.

2 F. J. Dyson, 'Time Without End: Physics and Biology in an Open Universe', *Reviews of Modern Physics*, vol. 51, no. 3, pp. 447–60, July 1979.

3 Islam, 'Possible Ultimate Fate of the Universe' (see note 1 above).

4 Dyson, op. cit. See also A. Berry, 'Time's Winged Chariot May Be Late Arriving', *Daily Telegraph*, 15 May 1981.

5 These two remarkable calculations were made by a London barrister, Mr R. O. Havery, in a letter to the *Daily Telegraph*, 20 May 1981.

6 Dyson, op. cit.

7 One of the best photographs of the galaxy Messier 87, also known as NGC 4486, appears in Plate 2 of the *Hubble Atlas of Galaxies*, by Alan Sandage (ed.), Carnegie Institute of Washington, Washington DC, 1961. See also a report in *Nature*, vol. 293, pp. 336–7, 1 October 1981, on extragalactic jets.

8 See, for example, R. Sheaffer, 'Are We Alone After All: The Pendulum Swings Back', *Spaceflight*, vol. 22, pp. 334–9, November 1980; M. H. Hart, 'An Explanation for the Absence of Extraterrestrials on Earth', *Quarterly Journal of the Royal Astronomical Society*, vol. 16, pp. 128–35, 1975. Also F. J. Tipler, see notes 3 and 4 to Chapter 14.

9 Dyson, op. cit.

Bibliography

N.B. In the case of two or more authors or editors, the book is listed under whichever is first in alphabetical order.

ADAMS, J. Mack and Douglas H. Haden (eds). *Social Effects of Computer Use and Misuse*, John Wiley, New York, 1976.

ALEKSANDER, I. *The Human Machine: A View of Intelligent Mechanisms*, Georgi Publishing, St Saphorin, Switzerland, 1978.

APTER, Michael J. *The Computer Simulation of Behaviour*, Hutchinson, London, 1970.

BANKS, Martin. *Living with the Micro*, Sigma Technical Press, Wilmslow, Cheshire, 1980.

BERRY, Adrian. *The Next Ten Thousand Years: A Vision of Man's Future in the Universe*, Cape, London, 1974; Coronet Books, London, 1976; Dutton, New York, 1974; New American Library, New York, 1975.

—— *From Apes to Astronauts*, *Daily Telegraph*, 1981.

BOBROW, D. G. and Allan Collins (eds). *Representation and Understanding: Studies in Cognitive Science*, Academic Press, New York, 1975.

BODEN, Margaret. *Artificial Intelligence and Natural Man*, Harvester Press, Hassocks, Sussex, 1977.

BRAND, Steward (ed.). *Space Colonies*, Penguin Books, London, 1977.

BRITISH INTERPLANETARY SOCIETY. *Project Daedalus: The Final Report on the BIS Starship Study*, published by the Society, 27–9 South Lambeth Road, Vauxhall, London, 1978.

BROWN, Richard Henry and Patrick Henry Winston (eds). *Artificial Intelligence: An MIT Perspective* (2 vols), Massachusetts Institute of Technology Press, Boston, 1979.

BUNDY, A. *Artificial Intelligence: An Introductory Course*, Edinburgh University Press, 1978.

BURKITT, Alan and Elaine Williams. *The Silicon Civilisation*, W. H. Allen, London, 1980.

CALDER, Nigel. *Spaceships of the Mind*, BBC Publications, London, 1977.

Bibliography

COLBY, Kenneth. *Artificial Paranoia: A Computer Simulation of Paranoid Processes*, Pergamon Press, Oxford, 1975.
—— and Roger Schank. *Computer Models of Thought and Language*, W. H. Freeman, San Francisco, 1973.
CROSSON, Frederick J. and Kenneth M. Sayre. *The Modelling of Mind: Computers and Intelligence*, Simon and Schuster, New York, 1963.
DALE, Ella and Donald Michie (eds). *Machine Intelligence* (2 vols), Oliver & Boyd, London, 1968.
DREYFUS, Herbert. *What Computers Can't Do: A Critique of Artificial Reason*, Harper & Row, New York, 1972.
ENGELBERGER, Joseph F. *Robots in Practice: Management and Applications of Industrial Robots*, Kogan Page, London, 1980.
EVANS, Christopher. *The Mighty Micro: The Impact of the Computer Revolution*, Gollancz, London, 1979.
FREY, Peter W. (ed.). *Chess Skill in Man and Machine*, Springer-Verlag, New York, 1977 and 1978.
GAINES, B. R. and E. H. Mamdani (eds). *Fuzzy Reasoning and its Applications*, Academic Press, London and San Francisco, 1981.
GARDNER, Martin. *Logic Machines, Diagrams and Boolean Algebra*, Dover Publications, New York, 1958.
GEDULD, Harry M. and Ronald Gottesman (eds). *Robots, Robots, Robots*, New York Graphic Society, Boston, 1978.
GEORGE, Frank. *The Brain as a Computer*, Pergamon Press, Oxford, 1961.
—— *Machine Takeover: The Growing Threat to Human Freedom in a Computer-Controlled Society*, Pergamon Press, Oxford, 1977.
—— and J. D. Humphries (eds). *The Robots are Coming*, NCC Publications, Manchester, 1974.
GOODSTEIN, R. L. *Development of Mathematical Logic*, New York Graphic Society, Boston, 1971.
GREENBLATT, Stanley. *Understanding Computers Through Common Sense*, Cornerstone Library, New York, 1979.
HEISERMAN, David L. *How to Build Your Own Computer-Controlled Robot*, Tab Books, Blue Ridge Summit, Pennsylvania, 1979.
HOFSTADTER, Douglas R. *Godel, Escher, Bach: An Eternal Golden Braid – A Metaphorical Fugue on Minds and Machines in the Spirit of Lewis Carroll*, Harvester Press, Hassocks, Sussex, 1979.

HOOK, Sidney. *Dimensions of Mind*, Collier-Macmillan International, New York, 1961.

HUBBARD, John I. *The Biological Basis of Mental Activity*, Addison-Wesley, Reading, Massachusetts, 1975.

INSTITUTION OF ELECTRICAL AND ELECTRONIC ENGINEERS. *Proceedings of the Fifth International Conference on Pattern Recognition, Miami Beach, Florida, December 1-4, 1980*, published in 1981 by the IEEE Computer Society, 10662 Los Vanqueros Circle, Los Alamitos, California, 90720; and by the IEEE Service Center, 445 Hoes Lane, Piscataway, New Jersey, 08854.

JACKSON, Philip C. *Introduction to Artificial Intelligence*, Petrocelli Charter, New York, 1975.

JARRETT, Dennis. *The Good Computing Book for Beginners*, EEC Publications, London, 1980.

KOWALSKI, Robert. *Logic for Problem-Solving*, North Holland Publishing, Amsterdam, 1979.

LANGER, Susanne K. *An Introduction to Symbolic Logic*, Allen & Unwin, London, 1937; Dover Publications, New York, 1937.

LAURIE, Peter. *The Micro Revolution*, Futura Publications, London, 1980.

LERNER, Laurence. *A.R.T.H.U.R. The Life and Times of a Digital Computer*, Harvester Press, Hassocks, Sussex, 1974.

LOOFBOURROW, Tod. *How to Build a Computer-Controlled Robot*, Hayden Book Co., Rochelle Park, New Jersey, 1977.

MCCORDUCK, Pamela. *Machines Who Think: A Personal Inquiry into the History and Prospect of Artificial Intelligence*, W. H. Freeman, San Francisco, 1979.

MADDISON, John. *National Education and the Microelectronics Revolution: An Annotated Bibliography and a Media Resources List*, Cleveland Printing Co., Cleveland, Avon, 1980.

MEYER, Carl and Hans Sagan. *Ten Easy Pieces: Creative Computing for Fun and Profit*, Hayden Book Co., Rochelle Park, New Jersey, 1980.

MICHIE, Donald. *Expert Systems in the Micro-electronic Age*, Edinburgh University Press, 1979.

—— (ed.) *Semantic Information Proceedings*, Massachusetts Institute of Technology Press, Boston, 1968.

MINSKY, Marvin. *Computation: Finite and Infinite Machines*, Prentice-Hall, Englewood Cliffs, New Jersey, 1967.

—— and Seymour Papert. *Artificial Intelligence Progress Report*, Massachusetts Institute of Technology Press, Boston, 1972.

169

Bibliography

MONOD, Jacques. *Chance and Necessity*, Random House, New York, 1971.

MOODY, Robert. *The First Book of Microcomputers*, Hayden Book Co., Rochelle Park, New Jersey, 1978.

O'NEILL, Gerard K. *The High Frontier: Human Colonies in Space*, Cape, London, 1977.

PORTER, Arthur. *Cybernetics Simplified*, English Universities Press, London, 1969.

RAPHAEL, Bertram. *The Thinking Computer*, W. H. Freeman, San Francisco, 1975.

REICHARDT, Jasia. *Cybernetics, Art and Ideas*, New York Graphic Society, Boston, 1971.

RENMORE, C. D. *Silicon Chips and You*, Sheldon Press, London, 1979.

ROSENBERG, Jerry M. *The Computer Prophets*, Collier-Macmillan International, New York, 1969.

SCIENTIFIC AMERICAN. *Information*, W. H. Freeman, San Francisco, 1966.

SIMON, Herbert A. *The Sciences of the Artificial*, Massachusetts Institute of Technology Press, 1970.

SMULLYAN, Raymond. *What is the Name of this Book?*, Prentice-Hall, Englewood Cliffs, New Jersey, 1978.

SPRACKLEN, Dave and Kathe. *Sargon: A Computer Chess Program*, Hayden Book Co., Rochelle Park, New Jersey, 1978.

SUSSMAN, Gerald Jay. *A Computer Model of Skill Acquisition*, American Elsevier, New York, 1975.

TAUBE, Mortimer. *Computers and Common Sense*, McGraw-Hill, New York, 1961.

VON NEUMANN, John. *The Computer and the Brain*, Yale University Press, New Haven, Connecticut, 1958.

WALTER, Russell. *Scelbi's Secret Guide to Computers*, Scelbi Publications, Elmwood, Connecticut, 1980.

WEIZENBAUM, Joseph. *Computer Power and Human Reason: From Judgement to Calculation*, W. H. Freeman, San Francisco, 1976.

WHITESIDE, Thomas. *Computer Capers: Tales of Embezzlement and Fraud*, New American Library, New York, 1978.

WIDERHOLD, Gio. *Database Design*, McGraw-Hill, New York, 1977.

WINOGRAD, Terry. *Understanding Natural Language*, Academic Press, New York, 1972.

WINSTON, Patrick. *Artificial Intelligence*, Addison-Wesley, Reading, Massachusetts, 1977.

WOOLF, Harry (ed.). *Some Strangeness in the Proportion: A Centennial Symposium to Celebrate the Achievements of Albert Einstein*, Addison-Wesley, Reading, Massachusetts, 1980.

WOOLRIDGE, Dean. *Mechanical Man – The Physical Basis of Intelligent Life*, McGraw-Hill, New York, 1968.

Index

colonisation, 134–5, 137–42, survival of, 147–8, von Neumann's propositions concerning, 132–4
survival: pattern recognition important in, 99; super-intelligent machines', 148

Tale-spin program, 81–3
tape cassettes, programs on, 33, 34
Taylor, Theodore, 137–8
telephone-call flowchart, 35–6
terminal, 153
theology, artificial intelligence and, 19–20
theorem, computer proof of, 30n
Thermodynamics, Second Law of, 131
Thinking Computer, The (Raphael), 92
Thomas Aquinas, St, 20n
thought: electronic, *see* artificial intelligence; immortal soul and, 19–20; human, artificial intelligence indistinguishable from, 3, 9, 14–16, 18–19, machine compared with, 3, 58–9, 67, 127–9
ticket reservation, computerised, 100, 111–12
time: beginning and end of, *see* Universe; small units of, 119
Tipler, Frank J., 134–5, 138, 139
tone of voice, *see* voice
travel agent: replacement by computer, 114
treachery, computer, 130
treasure, search for, 89–92

Tree of Knowledge, 85–6
tree search, 86, 88–91, 153
trickery, artificial intelligence faked by, 9–14, 75
truth, understanding not concerned with, 75
Turing, Alan, 14–15, 17, 18–19, 20, 22
Turing Test, 17–19, 153
2001: A Space Odyssey, 94, 115

Uncertainty Principle, 128–9
understanding, 75; computers educated in, 75–80; conceptual errors in, 109; contribution of sentence parsing to, 72–5; from different viewpoints, 75–7
Universe: beginning of, 143; collapse of (Big Crunch), 144, immense number of years until, 145–6, super-intelligent machines and, 144, 146, 147–9; ever-expanding, 144; fuel exhaustion in, 144–5, 147–8
unusual events: computer recognition of, 71

vision, 105–6; *see also* pattern recognition
voice, tone of, computer response to, 109–10
voice recognition, *see* speech recognition
von Neumann, John, 132–3
von Neumann machines, 132–3, 153; space colonisation by, *see* space exploration and colonisation

181